ORGANIZATION DEVELOPMENT FOR MANAGERS

ADDISON-WESLEY PUBLISHING COMPANY

Reading, Massachusetts
Menlo Park, California
London • Amsterdam
Don Mills, Ontario • Sydney

GLENN H. VARNEY *Bowling Green State University*

ORGANIZATION DEVELOPMENT FOR MANAGERS

 Printed in the United States of America. Published simultaneously in Canada. Library of Congress Catalog Card No. 77-73948.

0-201-07983-6
DEFGHIJKLM-MA-898765432

PREFACE

The strength, vitality, and progress of organizations depends in large measure on how creatively human resources are developed and utilized from both the individual's and the organization's viewpoints. Managers are faced with and engaged in an era of extreme pressure for change, for accelerating technological and societal changes lead to the need for new solutions to heretofore little-known problems within organizations. Such problems first emerge as a subtle dissatisfaction for work life, which often shows up in absenteeism, turnover, withdrawal, and resistance. As the desire for a different and oftentimes undefined way to live in an organization emerges, the pressures for change become more active. Managers often experience this need as open rebellion, questioning of management prerogatives, challenge of decisions, and refusal to work.

All in all, these problems are viewed by managers as frustrating challenges which must be met. Few, if any, competent managers would attempt to solve the problems facing them in any other manner than by seeking out ways to adapt their style to meet the challenge.

This book sets forth one way to meet the challenge. It outlines the new field of Organization Development and attempts to give managers a framework for studying their own organizations. Furthermore, it attempts to lay out some of the approaches and technology associated with the field of OD.

At the least a manager should be able to pick up more ideas on how to solve some day-to-day problems. At the most, this book may present a way to view the entire organization so that changes can be planned in a more systematic and effective manner.

Bowling Green, Ohio
May 1977

G.H.V.

CONTENTS

1

CHANGING ENVIRONMENT AND ORGANIZATION DEVELOPMENT

The following words were spoken by the president of a moderately large organization before his executive group.

> Good morning, gentlemen. I'm awfully glad that all of you could make it this morning. I've called this meeting to make a rather startling and very important kind of announcement to you as a group, one which I am confident you will find most interesting and useful in the total operation of our company. As some of you know, I just returned from a meeting of presidents of various organizations in New York City. The outgrowth of this meeting is that I have decided that we should adopt a slightly different approach to managing our company. I have found that many of our competing organizations and many companies of significance throughout the country are using a system of managing called Management By Objectives. The kinds of results these companies have gotten through the use of this plan are, to say the least, very startling. I can see no reason why we shouldn't introduce the MBO approach in our company and for that reason I've called this meeting this morning.
>
> My plan is that this go into effect next Monday morning. I will have in your hands at that time a statement of the basic goals and objectives of the company and will specifically indicate which areas each of you will have as your responsibility. I will spell out in some detail the objectives, in other words, that your organization will be accountable for. I would like to have you examine these objectives and have them back to me within ten days with your plans for implementing and reaching the objectives. An integral part of the system will be that we are going to have regular follow-up review meetings to see that these objectives are carried out and I plan to do this on at least a quarterly basis and I will give you further details later.
>
> Now remember the important thing about this is that we are going to set some very realistic, very workable, very practical goals which are going to help lead us to a very successful future in the next five to ten years. Each of you will benefit, of course, by receiving remuneration in direct relationship to the degree in which you accomplish your objectives. I'm counting on all of you to carry out your role in this. I have no doubts in my mind that we as a total organization will be highly successful in accomplishing our targets. I'll have all the details in your hands shortly. If

you have any questions, feel perfectly free to step into my office at any time. By the way, make arrangements with Mary when you do so. Thank you very much, gentlemen. I'll be looking forward to seeing you and particularly those detailed plans for accomplishment of our corporative objectives.

You will no doubt feel after reading the above that the president was entirely and arbitrarily wrong in his approach and perhaps foolhardy in the way he introduced Management By Objectives to his organization. Although this particular example may seem a bit unusual, the fact is that this change strategy is applied by many chief executives, managers, and supervisors in organizations every day. The difficulty with such a change strategy is that it oftentimes is not viewed in terms of the impact it has on the organization—and instead of desired change, the end result is usually resistance, conflict, and confusion for the organization.

In this case the president introduced a major change into his organization without any apparent awareness of the full impact that such an introduction and change was going to have on his organization. In fact, he gave very little consideration to the basic design of the change and the way in which he was going to introduce it relative to the receptivity and support which he would obtain from his officers and executives. Furthermore, he felt that he needed this change for reasons which most managers would normally view as unjustifiable. First of all, he thought it was necessary to make the change because he saw other organizations ("fellow presidents") changing and using this new concept of managing. Second, he apparently sensed a need for some kind of change in his organization.

What were the cues that he received that indicated to him that there was a need for such a program as Management By Objectives? In both introducing the change and sensing the need for it, he seemed unaware of and insensitive to his own organization and its needs.

The third point we'd like to make is that the organization responded directly in this particular situation with a mounting resistance to the president. As a matter of fact, by the end of six months he had received but two out of 12 plans for accomplishing the objectives which he requested. The remaining 10 individuals had found various excuses, reasons, and justifications for not submitting their plans. One might expect that if the president were aware of his dilemma, he would take a more authoritarian approach to solve it. In this case, however, he developed a sensitivity to his executives and began to listen to them.

Essentially what they told him was that the kind of strategy that he was introducing in the organization was going to create a major "stir"; and therefore resistance would flourish much as it did with the top executives. Their suggestions to him included a more systematic examination of the concept of Management By Objectives and the introduction of such a change, if it were necessary at all, on a gradual and transitional basis. They further suggested that people being asked to make the change be involved in the design of the strategy itself.

Following the suggestions of his executive group, he then found it possible to move ahead on a gradual basis. The sequel to this particular case problem is that today this organization has a flourishing Organization Development (OD) program under way which is used on an ongoing basis to manage the change that is necessary for the organization to survive in its current environment.

There was perhaps a time when the approach used by this president would have worked reasonably well. However, it is generally agreed that today such an approach would probably falter. What other factors then contributed to the situation which we face and why is it necessary for managers to view the changed process in organizations in a more systematic way? Or to put it another way, why is the field of Organization Development emerging at this time?

APPROACH USED IN THIS BOOK

The basic purpose of this book is to look at the process of change from a manager's viewpoint and to help managers think about how they bring about change in a systematic and orderly way. The entire field of Organization Development (OD) has emerged in direct response to the problems managers face in keeping up with the changes in our society and in the highly technical and ever-changing environment in which they find themselves. This manual will explore what OD is in a specific way, and, we hope, will help managers to understand what planned organizational change is. We will examine an overview of OD and look at it in a step-by-step approach. We will then move to a systematic way of recognizing the need for change in organizations which will involve how we collect data and how we understand the data relative to organizations (including how they function today and as they should function in the future). At the end of the Book we will be talking about how the planning and initiation of change should take place and how we should measure such change. We will conclude the book by looking at some OD techniques and strategies which are common in the field today and would be useful to managers. Finally, the last chapter will show how you can install your own OD program.

A WAY OF THINKING ABOUT CHANGE

> Dramatic forces of change are at work in our society today. There are signs of crisis in almost every major institution. Many of these center around people—the desire of individuals for a richer quality life in their everyday lives and on the job.
>
> Industrial concerns are subject to increasing pressures seeking improvement in the work force and in the environment. We hear a lot about blue collar blues, the dehumanization of workers, monotony on the assembly line, and worker alienation.
>
> Obviously, we in General Motors are concerned about the increasing criticism being directed toward the assembly line and other aspects of our business.*

Here is a statement from the largest corporation in the world expressing concern over what Stephen Fuller refers to as "dramatic forces of change at work in our society today." Such concern from a major corporation like General Motors surely is evidence that there is a need for systematically thinking about how we deal with the human resources in our organization rather than as we have done in the past—i.e., by oftentimes force-fitting the human organization to the mechanical and technical side of our business.

What does all of this mean to the manager who has to live with the management of human resources every day? As one organization (Saga Foods) puts it, "The concept of boss is to find the subordinates' needs and serve them."† Saga Foods' managers are taught to think in this way. They are no longer encouraged to think about themselves as leaders who have the right and power to direct and manage human resources. Why is such a change taking place in a company like Saga? Why is General Motors activating major organizational changes today? Why are hundreds of other organizations in this country, as well as

---

* Stephen H. Fuller, Vice President, General Motors Corp., February 8, 1973.

† *Business Week*, July 22, 1972.

in Europe and other nations around the world, looking at how they manage the human resources of their organization? As Stephen Fuller points out, it is basically due to the changing environment in which we find ourselves today.

Dr. Frank Friedlander (Case Western Reserve University) has provided a graphic way of thinking about this change, as shown in Fig. 1.1.

We shall look first at the social and technical environment. The technology of our society and the world today is increasing at a rapid rate. Many specialists estimate that we are doubling our technical know-how approximately every five years, and it is further estimated that by the end of another decade we will be doubling it every three and one-half to four years.

This kind of technology, growing out of the U.S. space program and the need for environmental protection, has created an enormous problem for organizations in terms of how they accomplish their tasks. There are many illustrations of the changes which technology is bringing about in organizations; probably OSHA represents one of the most immediate and far-reaching technical changes brought about by the need to protect the physical environment in which workers perform their tasks.

With the rapid change in technology, the tasks are constantly in the state of change also. In a similar situation several decades ago, it would have been simple to adjust to these changes as they occurred and force-fit the individual into the organization's needs.

Fig. 1.1 Influence of changing environments (By Dr. Frank Friedlander, Case Western Reserve University. Used by permission.)

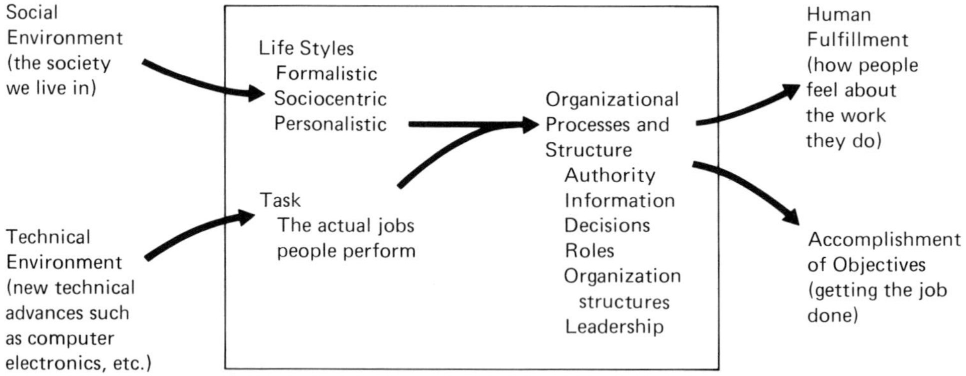

A further complication we face is that the social environment is also rapidly changing. Our society now includes a well-educated work force whose members are changing their values. And the work force is composed of increasingly younger people; it is estimated that approximately 50 to 55 percent of our work force is now under 28 years of age.

Basically what we find ourselves doing in organizations is moving from a group of people who have traditionally been formalistic in their life-style (i.e., who adhere strictly to prescribed forms or rules) to a social group more concerned with its own set of values and beliefs.

The term "life-style" refers to individuals in terms of their action and thoughts which are partly unique to them and partly shared by others. Thus a life-style is a product of one's own culture and deliberate choices. It is often thought of as being comprised of a number of dimensions. These dimensions represent various aspects of life which are likely to be dealt with in some way or another in all of our societies around the world. One dimension, for example, would be the nature of the relationship between father and son; another would be the meaning and significance of work.

Research has identified three basic classifications of life-styles. The earliest of these life-styles, referred to as *formalistic,* was prevalent around the turn of the century. This life-style, which still prevails today, emphasized rationality, control, and order in one's life. It developed along with, and was fostered by, the traditional, bureaucratic model of organization.

Generally, as technological changes became more rapid and organizations became more complex, a second life-style began to emerge. Shortly after World War II, people began to recognize the social nature of man. Within the behavioral sciences an entirely new field emerged called "group dynamics." Out of this social, interpersonal, group context was developed industrial humanism—or human relations, as we know it today. This new model of organization stressed personal growth, human dignity, work satisfaction, and democratic processes through various collaborative, interpersonal, and group relationships. It also fostered the *sociocentric* life-style.

After World War II, advances in technology for the production of goods and the communication of information led to a society which became a much more prosperous and much better informed society than ever known in the history of the world. This increase in wealth of information led to the emergence of a still different life-style, often referred to as the *personalistic* life-style. This particular life-style, accepted by many of our younger people today, is often idealistic and emphasizes personal choice and responsibility along with an integration of all aspects of one's life.

Dr. Thomas Bier constructed a description of each life-style (see Fig. 1.2) which compares the characteristics of the various life-styles for several different dimensions. It is interesting to look at these and reflect on how you feel about your own beliefs as they are compared with the formalistic, sociocentric, and personalistic life-styles.

Understanding that life-styles are in a rapid state of change will have a significant bearing on our ability to understand organizational problems. Such changes are predictive of the types of organizations we will have in the future. For example, there is a definite relationship between the structure and functions of an organization and the styles of living and working of the people in the organizations. Organizations are at least partially defined by the combined life-styles of the members of the organization. How people look at organizations and how they are constructed are results of the cultural changes that are taking place in our society. Once organization structure and the various processes within the structure are fairly well stabilized, they tend to foster or develop that style of life and form of man for which they were originally designed.

What this means is that a person moving into an organization begins to become socialized in terms of that structure. The way new people are added to an organization has considerable impact on the way that organization is designed. For instance, if an organization of 1000 people introduced 100 new members into the organization each year, it wouldn't take more than 5 to 10 years before the total value system of that organization would be changed. With the rapid increase of younger members in our work force, organizations are experiencing an acceleration of pressure to redefine and restructure the organization more in keeping with the newer life-styles which are becoming more prevalent.

From a manager's viewpoint, knowledge of changing life-styles is important. Managers must be aware of the expectations of new members of an organization who have life-styles different from the present members and realize they require different styles of managing. It is possible for managers to better understand what kinds of conditions need to be set up within their organizations in order for individuals to realize growth and development and to maximize their work effectiveness.

Fig. 1.2 Comparisons of characteristics of various life-styles (By Dr. Thomas Bier, Cleveland State University, Cleveland, Ohio. Used by permission.)

This chart describes how people will react or behave in certain situations when they hold different sets of values and beliefs.

Life-Style Dimensions	Formalistic	Sociocentric	Personalistic
Antecedent of action	Direction from authorities	Discussion, agreement with others	Direction from within
Form of control	Rules, laws, rewards, punishments	Interpersonal commitments	Action congruent with sense of self
Information for control	Rules, laws, authorities' wants	What "we" think and feel	What "I" think and feel
Object of responsibility	Superordinate powers	Peers, colleagues, self	Self
Desired end	Compliance	Consensus, agreement	Actualization of individual
To be avoided	Deviation from authoritative direction	Failure to reach agreement	Not being oneself
Material goods	Compete for means of control	Collaborate for means of control	Take for granted
Use of experience	Validate external order	Share for agreement and growth	Define self
Basis for growth	Following the established order	Interaction	Acting on awareness of self
Position relative to others	Member of hierarchy	Peer group member	Separate individual
Interpersonal relations	Structure oriented	Group oriented	Individual oriented
Time perspective	Future	Near future	Present

It is interesting to compare the life-style dimensions of other groups. It is quite likely, indeed highly predictable, that the organization of the future is being cast today in the life-styles of our young people and that managers can look to the present life-style dimensions of college students and younger people to gain some insight into the form of organization which will be most effective at managing people in the future.

The problem facing managers today is how to manage the change through the establishment of structures and processes in the organization which result in both the accomplishment of the task and the achievement of the organization's goals. At the same time an environment should be created in which human fulfillment is also derived by the individuals within the organization.

The purpose of this book is to help managers examine the organizational structures and processes in light of the changing social and technical environment so that the change which is needed can be brought about in a systematic way.

THE MANAGER IN A CHANGING ENVIRONMENT

In the preceding section we laid out a way of thinking about the new major forces impacting management today. It is even more useful to think about how the specific factors which are closer to home in our day-to-day management (such as EEOC, OSHA, inflation, environment, etc.) are affecting the way we manage.

We have outlined below a list of major contemporary social and environmental changes that are having an impact on how we manage our organizations. Beside each item is a place for you to score the extent to which each of these items affects you as you manage in your organization. As you read these items give yourself a score. In this way you can get a measure of the magnitude of change affecting you today. The scoring scale is as follows:

5 — Very heavy impact
4 — Fairly heavy impact
3 — Moderate impact
2 — Fairly light impact
1 — Very light impact
0 — No impact

The Manager in a Changing Environment*

Social impact changes since 1900 *Circle*

1. *Rapidly changing population* 0 1 2 3 4 5

   a. 1960 reached 179,000,000 in this country: 1970, 205,000,000; 1975, 212,000,000 to an estimated 233,000,000 by 1984. A slow rise.

---

* Hill, R., in *Impact: Your Organization and the Changing World,* R. Hill and Associates and Vanlynn and Associates, Jonesville, Mich. In press. Used by permission.

b. Took world from beginning of time until 1850 to go from 0 to 1 billion. But—

   1) From 1850 to 1975 we went from 1 to 4 billion.

   2) From 1975 to 1984 we will go from 4 to 5 billion.

c. 6% of the world's population (Americans) using 38% of world's resources.

d. Currently, the U.S. has taken the lead in moving toward zero population. In 1974 the birthrate index dropped to 1.91, below replacement of present population rate of 2.10.

e. However, if understanding and technology of overpopulation is not spread throughout the world, it is predicted by 2000 we will have

   Rich nations—from 1 billion now to only about 1.6 billion.
   Poor nations—from 2.4 billion now soaring to 5.4 billion.

f. Three recent developments may have an impact:

   The Pill.
   Abortion reform.
   Vast starvation problem in Asia and Africa.

2. *Changing age distribution* 0 1 2 3 4 5

a. Major shifts are occurring among various age groups, with significance for business and government. For example, young Americans between 20 and 34 represent more than half of the growth in U.S. population. They will sway the economy and set social trends for the next decade.

b. In world population, one of every three persons is below age 15.

c. Changes in values:

   Meaning of work and money
   Effect of affluence and mobility
   Single vs. married
   Sexual freedom

d. The trend of the rate of people over 45 is growing at twice the rate of people under 45.

e. 25% of our population is now over the age of 60. This promises a greater demand for apartments, medical care, luxuries such as fashionable clothing, books, recreation, and enriching educational opportunities.

f. What changing values will this trend bring?

3. *Variety of ethnic-cultural groups* 0 1 2 3 4 5

   a. Immigration groups:

      Chinese
      German
      Polish
      Irish
      Jewish
      Catholic
      Protestant
      California varieties
      Italian

   b. Black

      1) We grew up in a world where 1 in 10 was Negro. Today it is 1 in 6—and increasing by a 2-to-1 ratio.

      2) Rise of nationalism in the world and the Negro's struggle for identity in the U.S.

      3) Civil Rights agitation has made impact and change in America. The emergence of the new South where blacks are making huge strides—politically, economically, and socially.

4. *Prolonging of life* 0 1 2 3 4 5

   a. Life expectancy at the time of Christ—30 years. U.S. today—70+ years.

   b. Science very close to where average life span can be increased by many years—100 years. Substantial change in work and recreation patterns. All aspects of society will be affected.

   c. Already seeing the emergence of multiple careers.

   d. Major changes in life-styles are predicted.

   e. What is man? Should science intervene in the human process? Should there be genetic supermarkets of the future?

      Medical technology will link man with machinery, intensive care equipment, blood separators, detection equipment.

      Bio-engineering, where we will build modular bodies just as we now build modular homes:

         use of biofeedback
         new, specialized medical teams bring sophistication
         computerized medicine

laser beam surgery
stimulating brain centers with electric probes
drugs, memory, tranquilizers
organ transplants: heart, kidneys
bone marrow transplants for leukemia victims
heart pacers
Prosthetics
  bosoms
  teeth
  eyes
  limbs
  hair

f. Artificial insemination.
g. The ultimate is artificial intelligence—now being worked on in England.
h. Research telling us a great deal about how and why cells are born, age, and die.
i. New sources of nutrition.

5. *Urbanization and deurbanization* 0 1 2 3 4 5

a. By 1984 Calcutta will have 30 million.
   By 2000 Calcutta will have 50 million.
   We call these "Conurbations."
b. Asian cities planning for housing with densities of 4000 people per acre.
c. U.S. has its strip cities, but they are shrinking. Chicago, Philadelphia, New York and Detroit are smaller than 45 years ago. Loss of 850,000 people since 1970.
d. Why? Crime, taxes, poor schools and housing, racial strife.
e. Farm units: 1935—6,750,000
   1968—3,000,000
   and now going down at rate of 200,000 per year, declining at a rate of 1.4 million acres a year.

6. *Technological explosion* 0 1 2 3 4 5

a. St. Louis airport. Monsanto. 1968.
   "50% of what Monsanto will sell this year was not even invented 10 years ago."
b. Dupont. "90% of our sales this year not invented 20 years ago."

c. Estimate. "60% of what we will buy in a department store 10 years from now has not yet been discovered." Another way to look at this—18 cents of every dollar we'll spend 3 years from now is not on any shelf today.

d. 95% of all scientists who ever lived are alive today.

e. Half life of knowledge in physical sciences is now 9 years.

   Chemistry. If read 16 hours a day, at the end of a year would be 100 years behind.

   Technology has advanced more rapidly in the past 50 years than in the previous 5000.

f. 100 books a day are published.

g. New developments in telephone technology:

   Can now reach 250 countries and territories from almost any phone in America.

   70% of long distance calls are now relayed by a network of microwave towers, thus eliminating phone wires.

   Voices are now chopped up, converted to digital pulses by computerization, put back together at the receiving end in voice form—known as "pulse-code modulation."

h. New developments in television:

   Wall-sized screens.
   Interactive, two-way cable communication.
   Video disc players for home movies (biggest TV change since introduction of color).

i. New developments in communication:

   Seven Intelsat spacecraft orbit the earth, each with 4000 simultaneous circuits carrying voice, data and TV transmission.

   Mailgram via satellite costs half of phone conversation but more than first-class letter, yet is transmitted in half a day.

   Use of fiber optics for voice, video, and data transmission utilizes laser technology where a single strand (size of human hair) will handle 4000 simultaneous conversations.

7. *Students and education* 0 1 2 3 4 5

a. In 1939, 14% of our youth went to college.
   In 1969, 45% go to college.

b. 4,200,000 students in 1962.
   9,000,000 students in 1975.
   This does not include adults.

c. However, new trend is developing—a work experience gap between high school and college.

d. Another major trend developing—limiting classroom work to "real life" jobs.

   1969, there were 130 participating colleges.
   1975, there were 970 participating colleges with 180,000 participating students.

   Advantages are job-educational relevance, career head starts, career decisions and financial independence.

e. Monetary crisis in education:

   Cost is $108 billions and climbing with $ per pupil from $484 ten years ago to $1,255 today.

   Teacher salaries, a major factor in raising costs, in ten years is up an average of 85%.

   Uncertainty of government funds makes sound planning very difficult.

   In addition, lack of local taxpayer support has caused a rethinking of the operational needs by administrators and boards of education.

8. *Family makeup* 0 1 2 3 4 5

   a. Exclusion of all adults except parents from family. Whatever became of grandparents?

   b. Increased mobility: 36 million Americans move every year.

   c. Rising divorce, infidelity, the "singles" boom and communal designs are shaking the very roots of the traditional, nuclear family.

   d. As parents' influence fades, who's raising the children? No one, and as a result:

      One million kids run away from home each year.
      Suicide is second cause of death age 15–24.
      By age 17, one in ten women are mothers.
      By age 18, one of nine youths ends up in juvenile court.
      About 10% of all school-age children have moderate to severe mental and emotional problems.

e. Growing community of trained specialists in sex therapy, family counseling, marriage, and couples therapy.

f. Heavy emergence of communal groups of families:

A shelter against rootlessness and recession.
Makeup is middle-class, college educated.

g. Singlehood is rapidly emerging as the "new" respectable American life-style.

9. *Emergence of young and old in pressure groups* 0 1 2 3 4 5

a. The youth culture—affluent and outspoken with different values.

b. Makes up 21% of U.S. population ages 14–24.

c. Use of alcohol and marijuana by teenagers reaching epidemic proportions.

d. Become a legal adult at age 18.

e. Longer life expectance swells ranks of over 60.

f. Impact of senior citizens—impact of social security benefits and changing life-styles.

10. *Occupational changes* 0 1 2 3 4 5

a. Seventy years ago, only 3 in 10 workers were employed in service industries and 7 of 10 in production of goods. In 1970, 6 of every 10 were in services.

b. In 1970, white-collar workers outnumbered the blue-collar by more than 5 to 4.

c. In 1940 there were 3.9 million professional and technical employees and today it has grown to 12.9 million—twice the average labor force.

d. The growth rate of scientists and engineers has been triple that of the working population.

11. *Other interesting impact changes* 0 1 2 3 4 5

a. Three major technological developments in this century gave a big boost to our economy:

automobile
television
computer

b. The next ones may be:

space and ocean exploration
recreation
urban renewal
mass transit systems
hovercraft
environmental control
new forms of energy
electric and solar transportation systems
exotic, synthesized materials for building

c. Passing jobs:

coal miner
street car operator
elevator operator
street vendor
bootblack
restroom attendant
gondolier

d. More buildings constructed between 1945 and 1975 than in previous 6000 years.

Revolutions of our time

1. *Black revolution* 0 1 2 3 4 5

a. No longer are blacks listening to white liberals. Rather, they have forced a conscious reexamination of education, politics, manners, business practices, etc.

b. Centered around black power to affirm their distinctive ethnic background—black is beautiful—and demand its merit be recognized.

c. Long-term goals not substantially different from white except one does not have to act, dress, think and look like the WASP to achieve the goals.

d. Black children now have new and different images to model themselves after.

e. Substantially greater political impact. In 11 Southern states, only 72 blacks were elected to office in 1965 compared to 1560 now.

f. Still an economic problem—median income only $7808.

2. *Youth revolution of the 60s* 0 1 2 3 4 5
   a. Small minority were violent.
   b. Great majority not violent but grieved.
   c. Now in high schools.
   d. Display different value systems.
   e. Campuses are quiet and tired.

3. *Women's Lib revolution* 0 1 2 3 4 5
   a. The major revolution of our time with greater implications than the racial problem.
   b. Has strong legal support—from states to Congress and the President.
   c. Many emerging activist groups forcing compliance to strengthened civil rights legislation.
   d. About 25% of women employed in major companies are professional and technical employees.
   e. A profile:

      Comprise 51% of total U.S. population.
      87% are whites, 12% are blacks.
      Older than men on the average.
      Live longer than men by nearly 8 years.
      Women now own 47% of nation's wealth.
      One in 6 has a college degree, up from 1 in 10 a decade ago.
      47% of women 16 and older now work.
      Greater movement into traditionally male jobs.
      In law and medical schools, women now account for 20% of the enrollment compared to 5% ten years ago.

4. *Government intervention on rise* 0 1 2 3 4 5
   a. *General*
      1) Latest tally of federal regulators shows a total of 100,980 employees.
      2) Number of approved government forms has risen to 5146, requiring more than 130 million man hours a year to fill them out.
      3) Annual cost to the consumer is $2000 per family, or $130 billion nationwide.

4) Ralph Nader says: "Our unguided regulatory system undermines competition and entrenches monopoly at the public's expense."

b. *OSHA*

1) Many employers are inadvertent violators of the job safety and health act.
2) In first nine months OSHA conducted 22,868 inspections in 20,688 organizations employing 4,064,205 workers. Only 23% were found in compliance.
3) OCAW (Oil, Chemical and Atomic Workers), major oil companies signed comprehensive health and safety pacts. Has some loopholes, but is model for other labor agreements.

c. *EEO's new teeth*

1) Guidelines on sex discrimination are nearly accomplishing just about everything sought by women's rights groups:
   a) Minimum wages and premium pay for overtime.
   b) Special rest and meal periods or physical facilities.
   c) Same fringe benefits.
   d) Female employees receive same benefits as employee wives; i.e., maternity benefits.
   e) Pension or retirement plan must have same optional or compulsory retirement ages between sexes.
   f) No exclusion from employment because of pregnancy.
2) Over 200 companies and unions are now vulnerable because of resisting conciliation efforts.
3) Major impact on sports and education.
4) Newly emerging emphasis by Congress on age discrimination.
5) Must simply be regarded as a legitimate cost of doing business.

Major crises

1. *Energy crisis* 0 1 2 3 4 5

   a. U.S. has never designed a rational, long-range energy policy, despite that fuels account for a dollar value nearly equal to agriculture, food processing, and distribution.

b. The petroleum industry is short of domestic refining capacity by about 7,000,000 barrels per day.

c. Thus, the world's most advanced civilizations depend greatly on oil from countries generally considered weak, compliant, and disunited.

d. Needed is a huge R & D effort to find and refine new energy technology: nuclear, solar, tide, wind, geothermal.

2. *Shift in monetary power crisis* 0 1 2 3 4 5

a. The 1974 oil embargo by the OPEC nations, coupled by their swift price increase—$1.99/barrel to more than $10/barrel in 15 months—led to the greatest and swiftest transfer of wealth in all history.

b. The 13 OPEC countries earned $112 billion from the rest of the world in 1974 and increased this another 10% in 1975.

c. They could not spend it all and ran up payment surplus of $60 billion; thus, the international financial system was badly shaken.

d. At their current rate of accumulation, OPEC could buy out all companies on the world's major stock exchanges in 15.6 years.

3. *Self-identity crisis* 0 1 2 3 4 5

a. A fundamental change in the relationship between man and his environment is emerging. Source is the rise of massive technology.

b. The balance of power between man and the rest of nature has shifted and the emphasis is now moving from technology itself to the men who use it.

c. In government, fiscal and monetary instruments are used to control the level of economic activity which then repeals what was once called "laws of supply and demand."

d. Managers must now supervise the design of new products, create distribution networks and study consumer behavior in months rather than acting out a lifetime learning path in a traditional industry.

e. Even the educated and affluent must now choose among the many roles and identities available to them.

f. Not only are teenagers afflicted with finding self, but the discontinuities of the world create a climate where men are burdened through middle age with doubts and questions about self.

g. Continuing and more intensive search for quality of life.

4. *The losing battle against crime in America* 0 1 2 3 4 5

a. Crimes of violence up 47% in past 5 years.

1) Identified as murders, forcible rapes, robberies, aggravated assaults.

2) Youngsters under 18 accounted for
11% murders
20% rapes
34% robberies
17% aggravated assaults

b. Crimes against property up 37% in past 5 years.

1) Identified as burglaries, larceny thefts, auto thefts.

2) Youngsters under 18 accounted for
54% burglaries
56% auto thefts
48% larceny thefts

c. Crimes by women have nearly doubled in past 10 years—up 82%.

1) Becoming more violent: robbery up 306%, aggravated assaults up 134%, murder is up.

2) In crimes against property: burglary up 246%, auto thefts up 162%, and larceny thefts up 404%.

3) Throughout the world, crime by women is on the rise.

4) Revolutionary terrorism has attracted women in growing numbers.

5) Crime is heaviest in Western states and metropolitan areas but rapidly on the increase in smaller cities and rural areas.

6) Increasing numbers of businesses are stolen blind. The cost is $21 billion: shoplifters, employees, a few customers.

7) Political terrorism on the rise throughout the world as underground arsenals were building for the Bicentennial Year.

8) Trend of private citizens organizing in various ways against crime.

9) Weak and bogged-down courts to blame for some of the increase in crime.

Emerging impact forces

1.	Change in moral values	0 1 2 3 4 5
2.	High level of expectations—affluence—median income over $12,000	0 1 2 3 4 5
3.	Transition from industrial society to post-industrial society	0 1 2 3 4 5
4.	Consumer protection	0 1 2 3 4 5
5.	An American athletic binge—as participants and spectators	0 1 2 3 4 5
6.	Growth of cultural centers	0 1 2 3 4 5
7.	Continuing education, a lifetime process	0 1 2 3 4 5
8.	Growing disparity between centralized planning and decentralized planning	0 1 2 3 4 5
9.	Raw material shortages	0 1 2 3 4 5
10.	Health care crisis	0 1 2 3 4 5
11.	Emergence of substantial worldwide trade	0 1 2 3 4 5
12.	Yearning for the "good ole days"	0 1 2 3 4 5
13.	Comeback for "mainline" religion	0 1 2 3 4 5
14.	World futures planning task forces	0 1 2 3 4 5
15.	Megafamines—10–15 million people starving to death	0 1 2 3 4 5
16.	Growing polarity between "haves" and "have-nots"	0 1 2 3 4 5
17.	Lack of confidence in major institutions	0 1 2 3 4 5
18.	American Indians become new minority force	0 1 2 3 4 5
19.	World recession and inflation	0 1 2 3 4 5
	Your score (total of all circled numbers)	
	Total possible score	190

The maximum score you can receive is 190. If your score leans toward the high side, you are feeling the effect of social changes in the way you manage. You are a person who will probably find the ideas, concepts, and techniques outlined in this book helpful in your work.

CONCLUSIONS

We hope that you have reached the conclusion, as we have, that change is inherent in our work life today. This change is, in fact, speeding up and becoming more difficult to manage than it has been in the past. Finally, we hope that you, the manager, will recognize the need to more systematically learn how to manage change in order to bring about a more orderly process that is acceptable both to the human organization and the technical requirements of the business. Matching the needs of human beings to the structures and technology of the organization is what this book is all about.

2

WHAT IS ORGANIZATION DEVELOPMENT?

At no time since the Industrial Revolution have society's attitudes, values, and beliefs about work and the work force—and their relationship to organizations—undergone such intensive scrutiny, debate, and change. Evidence of this change is all about us and has been recorded and discussed in a flood of articles, books, and reports.* One of the most recent expositions on this subject expresses the situation this way:

> Because work is central to the lives of so many Americans, either the absence of work or employment in meaningless work is creating an increasingly intolerable situation. The human cost of this state of affairs is manifested in worker alienation. But the essential first step toward these goals is the commitment on the part of the policy maker in business, labor, and government to the improvement of the quality of work life in America.†

In general, American managers are faced with changing the cultural influences that relate to how people work in organizations. To the dismay of many managers, they find that their knowledge, skills and techniques are not in tune with what has been described by Dr. Allan Filley as the second "Great Age of Social Experimentation." They are faced with acquiring new managerial competencies and skills which involve learning to manage in a way which successfully influences a changing human work force seeking a quality work life. Thus in virtually every modern organization, those persons charged with responsibility for human resource management are seeking improved and new skills as well as a better understanding of the complex and changing relationships of human behavior in organizations.

One of the visible recent responses is the emergence of Organization Development (OD) as a framework for study within which professional managers, researchers, and academics alike can come to grips with the complexities involved in organizing and managing human resources. Four factors are involved in the evolving practice of OD:

1. It is long-range effort to introduce planned change on a diagnosis which is shared by the members of an organization.
2. An OD program involves an entire organization or a coherent system or parts thereof.

---

* Appendix I is a bibliography of the literature associated with Organization Development.

† "Work in America." *Report of Special Task Force to the Secretary of Health, Education and Welfare* (Cambridge, Mass.: M.I.T., 1973).

3. Its goal is to increase organization effectiveness and enhance organizational choice in self-renewal.
4. The major strategy of OD is to intervene in the ongoing activities of the organization, facilitate learning, and to make choices about alternative ways to proceed.*

Like other more familiar areas that comprise the existing field of management practices, OD is based squarely on a variety of knowledge, skills, and experience. It is firmly rooted in such disciplines as psychology, organization behavior, and sociology.

The bulk of the literature applicable to OD is drawn from a variety of subject areas, such as:

History of organization behavior
Organization theory
Decision-making processes
Organizational communication
Nature and impact of technology
Behavioral analysis
Perceptual processes
Learning process theory
Motivational theory
Personality development
Informal organization
Organization structure
Interpersonal dynamics
Sociology
Organizations as systems
Organizational effectiveness
Role theory
Power and authority
Leadership
Organization environment
Small-group theory

In summary, the combined needs being forced upon organizations from societal changes require managers in organizations to be more aware, more responsive, and more able to bring about change in the ac-

* John J. Sherwood, *An Introduction to Organization Development.* Experimental Publication System, American Psychological Association, Issue 11 (1971).

complishment of the organization's basic objectives and tasks as well as meeting the desire for human fulfillment now being expressed throughout American society.

A DEFINITION OF OD

One of the most difficult things in compiling a manual on Organization Development is defining it exactly, so that the person unfamiliar with OD will have a sense of what it is and what it can do. There are at least four well-accepted definitions:

1. OD is a planned change effort evolving the total system managed from the top to increased organizational effectiveness through planned interventions using behavioral science knowledge. (Richard Beckhart)
2. Using knowledge and techniques from the behavioral sciences, Organization Development attempts to integrate individual needs for growth and development with organizational goals and objectives in order to make more effective organizations. (National Training Laboratories Institute)
3. OD is a process of planned organizational change which centers around a change agent who in collaboration with a client's systems attempts to apply valued knowledge from the behavioral sciences to client problems. (Warren Bennis)
4. Achieving an idea of corporate excellence to strive toward and perfecting a sound system of management which can convert driving into action. (Blake and Mouton)

The key words in these four definitions are:

Planned change
Total company
Increased organizational effectiveness
Interventions
Behavioral science knowledge
Individual needs/company goals
Change agent

It seems clear from these definitions that the one main element is the word "change." To put it another way, it involves looking at the organization and helping the organization to change in the direction it desires to go. There are many changes that are taking place in organizations all the time; however, most of these changes, except perhaps technical changes, are met frequently on a less than well-thought-out basis. The difficulty in organizations today is that our "let it happen as it may" strategy for change has caused problems in management of our human resources.

What OD does is look at change in terms of a planned and systematic approach involving major variables in the organization. Its basic objective is to increase the organization's ability to perform its tasks and meet its goals.

In OD terminology, such a planned change for the total organization is called an "intervention." Basically, OD attempts to make use of the knowledge found in the social and behavioral sciences. It has as one of its underlying themes the matching of individual needs or goals to the objectives and goals of the organization. The "change agent," as referred to in the Organization Development field, is the person who serves as the catalyst or prime mover of the change strategy. The change agent may be an internal consultant, a manager, or an external change agent. For purposes of our discussion in this context, think of yourself, the manager, as a change agent. We believe every manager is responsible in some way for bringing about change in the organization, and therefore is the most likely person to be involved in OD.

One major corporation in the United States which has an Organization Development program defines its OD approach as a "plan for applying appropriate resources to organization revitalization." It says, "It is a planned intervention in the ongoing management process with the explicit intent of applying new knowledge, new technology, new resources, and new individual organizational authenticity to the achievement of the organization's goals in a dynamic and uncertain environment." It furthermore states that the objective of the program is to "increase earnings now" and "to do so in such a way that the organization's capacity for continued growth and earnings is within its own control."

In addition, it states that the program is "a means of changing the management process from one of dependence on previous experiences to one of autonomy based on the utilization of total technical and human resources." This particular company does not think of OD as a programmatic effort. On the contrary, they see it as management in an organization renewal effort being conducted on a continuing basis over an extended period of time.

THE HISTORY OF OD

Dr. Wendell French (University of Washington) describes the early history of OD as follows:*

> Organization development programs emerged about 1957 and have at least three origins. One origin centers around the late Douglas McGregor's work with Union Carbide in an effort to apply some of the concepts and insights from laboratory training to a large system.
>
> The second origin centers around a headquarters human relations research group at the Esso Company. About the same year Douglas McGregor was beginning to work with Union Carbide, the Esso group began to view itself as an internal consulting group offering services to field managers—rather than as a research group writing reports for top management. In addition, with the help of Robert Blake and Herb Shepard, this group began to offer laboratory training in the refineries of Esso.
>
> Certainly a third origin of OD stems from the experience that researchers were gaining at the Survey Research Center at the University of Michigan in the use of attitude surveys and in feeding back survey results in an effort to change organizations. For example, Howard Baumgartel reported some research in 1959 which, in retrospect, was an article of very good insight on OD. In his conclusions he stated,
>
> "The results of this experimental study lend support to the idea that intensive group discussion procedure for utilizing the results of an employee questionnaire survey can be an effective tool for introducing positive change in a business organization. It may be that the effectiveness of this method, in comparison to traditional training courses, is that it deals with the system of human relationships as a whole (superior and subordinate can change together) and it deals with each manager, supervisor, and employee in the context of his own job, and his own problems, and his own work relationships."
>
> At the present time, OD efforts are becoming visible in England, Norway, Sweden, Holland, Japan, Canada and perhaps other

---

* French, W., "A Definition and History of Organization Development: Some Comments," *Proceedings of the 31st Annual Meeting of the Academy of Management,* Atlanta, Ga., Aug. 15–18, 1971. Used by permission.

countries, as well as in the United States. They are appearing in a wide range of kinds of institutions, including business firms, schools, police departments, and hospitals.

Some of the typical business organizations now heavily engaged in OD activities include such companies as: American Airlines, Armstrong Cork Company, Bankers Trust Company, Corning Glass Works, First National Stores, Genesco Incorporated, General Motors, Procter & Gamble, Texas Instruments, TRW Systems, Abbott Laboratories, Bank of New York, Celanese Corporation, Exxon Corporation, Federated Department Stores, Hotel Corporation of America, Imperial Chemical, ITT, Jewel Companies, Inc., Lever Brothers, NBC, Polaroid Corporation, Chrysler Corporation, Saga Food Service, and Donnelly Mirrors, Inc.

TYPICAL TERMS USED IN OD

One of the advantages of providing a list of terms is that it helps a person come to grips with and to understand what a new field is attempting to accomplish. In fact, it speeds up the training of new people by stimulating greater perception in understanding the concept of OD. The list of terms found in Appendix II was composed by Dr. Peter B. Vaill (George Washington University) and is representative of the typical language used by professionals in OD. Managers who decide to proceed with an OD effort will find these terms to be most useful.

IS OD DIFFERENT FROM OTHER PERSONNEL ACTIVITIES?

A typical question asked by managers is, "How is Organizational Development different from other personnel activities?" The easiest way to show the difference is to contrast other types of personnel activities such as manpower planning, recruiting and selection, managerial and supervisory development. We look at the goals, the scope, the signs of how these particular programs fail, strategies for correcting systems failure, processes and activities that are used, typical problems encountered, the kind of time frames that the programs work under, organizational initiative (where does the impetus come from?) and the capability of specialists required to perform the functions. We have summarized these differences in Fig. 2.1.

Fig. 2.1 Manpower resource management—functional interdependency (a description of how various manpower functions interrelate to support an effective program of manpower resource management)

Dimension	OMP Organization and Manpower Planning	OD Organization Development	RS Recruitment and Selection	MD Manager Development	MD Manpower Development
1. Goals	1. Relate and design organization to meet growth plans and changing environmental conditions to assure that organization will be able to accomplish its future objectives. 2. Assess present manpower strength/weaknesses in light of future manpower requirements with the objective of providing the needed talent to accomplish future objectives.	1. Improve organization effectiveness. 2. Utilize manpower resources more fully. 3. Facilitate change. 4. Manage conflict (internal and external). 5. Provide system for evaluating effectiveness of organization and its components.	1. Improve organization effectiveness. 2. Continuous supply of needed skills and talent (ability) required to man the organization today and in the future. 3. Provide internal inventory of manpower resources.	1. Improve organization effectiveness. 2. Identify high potential manager. 3. Develop high potential manager. 4. Provide adequate supply of managers.	1. Improve organization effectiveness. 2. Provide needed skills today and in the future. 3. Utilize and develop total manpower resources more fully.
2. Scope	Total organization and its components	Total organization and its components	Total organization and its components	Managers (as distinguished from supervisors; i.e., responsible for significant part of business—middle to top)	Total organization and its components

3. Signs of system failure	1. Falling behind competition 2. Organizationa conflict 3. Profit decline 4. Shortage of manpower (i.e., managers) 5. Obsolete skills 6. Shortage of manpower in general	1. Falling behind competition 2. Slow to change (slow on feet) 3. Organization conflict (internal/external) 4. Profit decline 5. Lack of organization thrust (i.e., motivation)	1. Low acceptance ratios 2. High recruitment costs 3. Poor public image	1. Lack of manager replacement 2. High turnover of managers 3. Ineptness of managers (mistakes)	1. Inadequate skills 2. High turnover 3. Lack of identification with organization goals
4. Strategy for correcting systems failure	1. Organization structure diagrams 2. Manpower audit and analysis	1. Organizational diagnosis 2. Organizational confrontation of problems	1. Design revision of strategy around OD diagnosis.	1. Design MD activities around OD diagnosis.	1. Design MD activities around OD diagnosis.
5. Processes and activities used	1. Reorganization—restructuring 2. Management systems change 3. Policy modification 4. Long-range planning	1. Confrontation meeting 2. Team building 3. Action research 4. Survey feedback 5. Intergroup problem solving	1. Confrontation meeting 2. External/internal environmental research 3. Survey feedback external/internal	1. Courses, conferences 2. Coaching 3. Job rotation 4. Manager assessment programs 5. Career paths	1. Courses, meetings 2. Communication media 3. Participative techniques

(*Cont.*)

Dimension	OMP Organization and Manpower Planning	OD Organization Development	RS Recruitment and Selection	MD Manager Development	MD Manpower Development
6. Typical problems encountered	1. Unpredictable organizational consequences 2. Shortages of manpower 3. Unsatisfactory manpower forecasting techniques lead to inaccurate forecasting.	1. Management failure to recognize need of OD approach to Manpower Resource Management 2. High degree of suspicion of OD 3. Inadequate techniques/tools 4. High cost	1. Failure to provide resources to attract good people 2. Inability of management to recognize cost of ineffective recruitment 3. Lack of global approach to problems	1. Unwillingness to invest in MD 2. Failure to identify contributing managers 3. Inability to identify developmental needs 4. Manager resistance 5. Lack of useful techniques for MD	1. Unwillingness to invest in MD 2. Inability to identify developmental needs 3. Poorly designed, ill-conceived program
7. Time frame	Continuous	Continuous	Continuous	Continuous	Continuous
8. Organizational initiative	Top executives Personnel executive All managers Consultants	Top executives Personnel and OD executives All managers Consultants	Top executives Personnel executives All managers	Top executives Personnel and OD executives All managers Consultants	Personnel and OD executives All employees Consultants
9. Capabilities of specialists required.	Organization analyst Consultant Planner Statistician Operation research skills	OD diagnostician Consultant Catalyst	Systems analyst Decision maker Evaluator Salesman	Diagnostician of MD needs Designer of programs	Diagnostician of needs Designer of programs Teacher

The main characteristics of the Organization Development effort which makes it different from other types of personnel activities is that it tends to be conducted on a broader basis, involving a larger segment of the organization and requiring a different kind of knowledge base from the other types of activities.

A CASE EXAMPLE

The president of a moderate-sized organization called his top executives together one day to discuss what he considered to be a major problem in the way in which they worked together. He pointed out that in their meetings he felt it necessary to push for answers and to pry information out of the officers. Generally, he did not feel that there was a free flow of information. He requested the members of the group to discuss this with him and to share their ideas and reactions.

The net effect of this request was that no one was willing to do this with the exception of one man. Following the meeting he came to the president and said that he felt it was something much deeper than could be seen by simply raising the question. The president was confused by this and asked what he meant. The officer said, "I believe that there are some things about the way we work together and, in particular, the way in which you manage with us that keeps us from talking freely and openly with each other."

The president reacted somewhat defensively to this comment. However, he was willing to entertain the possibility that such a problem could exist. The question then arose, "How do we deal with this?" It was suggested that what was needed was someone to help define the problem. They looked around to see if there was such an individual in the organization and decided that there was not. They then approached a nearby university which had a reputation for helping organizations solve such problems and found two members from the faculty of the university who agreed to work with the organization.

After a series of seven meetings with the top management group the conclusion was reached that the difficulty stemmed from two main sources; first, from the way the president interacted with his top officers. In a very quiet and subtle way, he was an extremely authoritarian type of leader and did not really come across as inviting comments from his staff. This had the general effect of inhibiting members of his executive group. Second, it was discovered that two members of the executive group, the vice-president of sales and the vice-president of operations, were constantly at odds with each other. This internal combat carried on through the organization, involving other people.

This discovery led to an action plan (a strategy) for changing this condition. The president would conduct, on a regular basis, a critique of meetings on various activities going on in the organization. As a standard part of every meeting he and members of the executive group would take a look at how well they were functioning together by sharing information about their perceptions of one another.

The other problem was dealt with directly by the two vice presidents who did not get along with each other. They went "off site" for a day and hammered out a working relationship designed to develop a greater understanding of how they worked together and how they could function more effectively together.

The result became quite apparent to members of the executive group and to other members of the organization as reports began to trickle in indicating that the change was noticeable. This change resulted in a more effective and efficient organization where things got accomplished more expeditiously.

Although this is a fairly typical OD intervention, it represents a macro (large system) approach where we are dealing with a total organization. Many OD activities are down further in the organization and deal with more minute (micro) parts of the organization. For example, it might be possible for a manager in a department to consider development of ways in which staff members can function in a more "synergistic" way. The manager's OD effort might be aimed primarily at finding ways to bring together a group of people to generate ideas as opposed to having it done on an individual basis. Another illustration might be the simple resolution of conflict between two individuals carrying a major responsibility in the organization. In other words, OD, is not limited just to the total organization but can be used down to a micro level where perhaps one person is at odds with another.

HOW DO YOU EXPLAIN TO OTHERS WHAT OD IS?

One of the difficulties of working in the field of Organization Development is trying to explain it to other people—and one way to explain what OD is would be to answer the following questions:

1. What forces at work on us in our organizations today are increasing the rate of change required of managers?

2. What other ways have we usually used to bring about change in our organizations?
3. Do we plan organizational change as systematically and conscientiously as we do technical and process type changes?
4. Do we spend as much time on organizational changes as we do on other types of changes in the organization?
5. What would be the best way to bring about change?
   a) To impose change on people.
   b) To involve other people in the change.
   c) To get people to give us their ideas and then make the decision ourselves.
6. What portion of a manager's time is used in making changes in the organization (or advising others)?
7. Would it be more helpful to have a more systematic way to bring about change than the one we currently use?

One other way that you might think about Organization Development is to complete the following brief quiz prepared by Dr. Warner Burke. The net effect of being able to answer the 25 questions correctly is that you will have some basis of knowledge and ideas about OD (once you know the correct answers), and will be able to discuss it reasonably intelligently with others. A scoring key follows the questionnaire.

So You Think You Know OD—by Dr. W. Warner Burke*

There are certain risks involved in putting together a piece such as this. Who am I to be doing the testing? There is a certain amount of arbitrariness; some of the items are ambiguous, others subject to opinion, and the selection of subjects reflects my own biases. But, given

---

I would like to express my appreciation to three of my colleagues—David Bradford, Jerry Harvey, and Harvey Hornstein—for their help on an earlier draft of this paper. I am also indebted to two groups—participants in the 1971–72 OD training program of Boston University's Human Relations Center and participants in the "Organization Development for Religious and Volunteer Systems," program sponsored by the Mid-Atlantic Training Committee and the Center for a Voluntary Society of NTL Institute—for providing a "test run" of an earlier 25-question sample.

* Burke, W. W., "So You Think You Know OD," *OD Practitioner* **4,** 2 (1975). Used by permission.

these risks, if I can stimulate you to think more about OD, possibly in a different way, then I have accomplished my purpose. And, if you don't like this test, you might have fun creating one of your own. If you do, send it to me; I'll be glad to try and pass it.

1. Engineering is to physics as OD is to
   a) business administration
   b) organization behavior
   c) the humanities
   d) psychology
   e) operations research
2. Which of the following types of change technology would be least appropriate as an OD intervention?
   a) Training in management by objectives
   b) Intergroup (or interdepartmental) conflict/problem-solving session
   c) Personnel research study advocating new organizational structure
   d) Team building
   e) Survey feedback
3. To be categorized as an OD intervention, a change event or activity should meet all but which one of the following criteria?
   a) Is a planned event or activity.
   b) Is determined by the manager of the client organization.
   c) Responds to a felt need on the part of the client group.
   d) Involves the client group in the planning and implementation of the event or activity.
   e) Leads to normative change in the organization's culture.
4. OD is best described by the word
   a) program
   b) process
   c) laboratory
   d) exercise
   e) project
5. OD is probably related most strongly to
   a) the Protestant ethic
   b) socialism
   c) democracy
   d) humanism
   e) industrialism

6. T Group is to experience-based education as OD is to
   a) operations research
   b) training
   c) applied behavioral science
   d) the scientific method
   e) sociology
7. Which organization has probably maintained the longest OD effort to date?
   a) TRW Systems
   b) YMCA
   c) Esso Research and Engineering
   d) Union Carbide
   e) Episcopal Church
8. From an OD perspective, which of the following academic institutions fits the grouping *least* well?
   a) UCLA
   b) MIT
   c) Carnegie Institute
   d) Case Western Reserve
   e) University of New Hampshire
9. Using as a criterion a person's membership in an OD "professional" organization, approximately how many people in the U.S. would categorize themselves as OD practitioners?
   a) 500
   b) 1000
   c) 1500
   d) 2500
   e) 5000
10. Which name fits in the following list *least* well?
    a) Shepard
    b) Schein
    c) Blake
    d) Drucker
    e) Beckhard
11. Considering the past research, theory and principles on which current OD is based, which of the following names fits *least* well?
    a) Lewin
    b) McGregor

c) Mayo
d) Roethlisberger
e) Rogers

12. 9.9 is to Blake as System 4 is to
    a) Bennis
    b) Trist
    c) Likert
    d) McGregor
    e) Lewin

13. The theorist(s)/practitioner(s) who deal(s) with change in organizational structure is (are)
    a) Argyris
    b) Blake and Mouton
    c) Herzberg
    d) Likert
    e) Lawrence and Lorsch

14. Which of the following is *not* part of Blake and Mouton's six-phase approach to OD?
    a) conflict utilization
    b) team development
    c) laboratory training
    d) developing an ideal strategic model
    e) intergroup development

15. "Interpersonal Competence and Organizational Effectiveness" is associated most with
    a) Beckhard
    b) Argyris
    c) Tannenbaum
    d) Schein
    e) Shepard

16. If you were using Likert's principles of organizational behavior as your basic parameter for diagnosing and changing an organization, which of the following would you choose as your objective for developing the review and control functions?
    a) Review and control done at all levels with lower units at times imposing more vigorous reviews and tighter controls than top management.

b) Review and control done at all levels with all units having equal responsibility.
c) Moderate downward delegation of review and control processes; lower as well as higher levels perform these tasks.
d) Relatively highly concentrated, with some delegated control to middle and lower levels.
e) Highly concentrated in top management.

17. Process consultation is to Schein as third-party consultation in conflict resolution is to
    a) Walton
    b) Lawrence
    c) Argyris
    d) Davis
    e) Bennis

18. Which of the following periodicals has the *least* relevance to OD?
    a) *Organizational Dynamics*
    b) *Harvard Business Review*
    c) *Journal of Applied Behavioral Science*
    d) *Psychology Today*
    e) *Training and Development Journal*

19. A "force field analysis" is
    a) an examination of process in a small group
    b) an examination of process in an organization
    c) a system for analyzing an organization's or group's environment and culture
    d) a technique for analyzing a problem situation with change as an objective
    e) a procedure for effective utilization of conflict

20. Job enrichment is to motivation theory as behavior modification is to
    a) reinforcement theory
    b) field theory
    c) conflict management theory
    d) Gestalt theory
    e) psychoanalytic theory

21. The concept which best describes the OD consultant's "approach" or model is
    a) systems analysis

b) laboratory method of learning
c) social intervention
d) sociotechnical
e) action-research

22. You, an OD specialist, have been asked to conduct an off-site, team-building meeting and you've learned that the present team leader has just been fired. What action should you take?
    a) Try to arrange for the leader to remain on the job until the meeting is completed.
    b) Demand to know why he was fired and why you were not involved or, at least, informed well in advance.
    c) Conduct the meeting with the team but without the leader.
    d) Arrange to conduct an "exit" interview with the former team leader and begin the process of diagnosing the reason(s) for his being fired with an eye toward getting him either reinstated or relocated in the organization.
    e) Temporarily withdraw from the contract and explain that it would be better to wait until the new leader is "on board."

23. Which of the following objectives is most likely to be an objective of MBO (Management By Objectives) as well?
    a) To build trust among individuals and groups throughout the organization.
    b) To create an open, problem-solving climate throughout the organization.
    c) To make competition more relevant to work goals and to maximize collaborative efforts.
    d) To make "process" just as legitimate as "content."
    e) To increase self-control and self-direction for people within the organization.

24. "Organization Mirror" is an OD technique that is most closely associated with which of the following categories of OD technology?
    a) team building
    b) intergroup
    c) survey feedback
    d) job enrichment
    e) training

25. Assuming that your only intervention is an off-site, team-building effort of four days with an ongoing organization workgroup, which of the following outcomes is *least* likely?

a) The level of problem-solving effectiveness is increased.
b) Mutual influence among team members is increased.
c) The level of intragroup trust is increased.
d) Personal involvement and participation in team meetings are increased.
e) The general evaluation by the members of the team meetings remains the same.

Scoring for "So You Think You Know OD"

Subcategories within the test:

Basic understanding of OD—1 through 6
General knowledge of OD—7, 8 and 9
Literature of OD—10 through 18
Technology of OD—19 through 25

These groupings are not "pure" by any means; there is overlap. By looking at the test in terms of these groupings, however, you may determine where your gaps are or, at least, where you and I disagree the most.

1. (b) Engineering is usually referred to as the applied part of physics. Similarly, Organization Development may be viewed as the applied arm of organizational behavior. Graduate courses in Organization Development are usually taught in a Department of Organization Behavior which is commonly located in a School of Business Administration.
2. (c) As I conceptualize the world of OD, there are at least three criteria for calling an intervening event in the life of an organization an OD intervention: (1) it responds to a felt need on the part of the client; (2) it leads to a planned process of normative or cultural change; (3) it involves the client in the planning and implementation.

   The response which seems to fit these criteria least well is the personnel research study. This response implies that a study was conducted and a change recommended without the persons to be affected having any involvement in its planning. Any of the other responses for item 2 could, of course, be handled in the same manner, but they do not so strongly imply a lack of collaboration with the group to be affected by the change.
3. (b) There is validity in all of the responses for this item. However, (b) is only partially correct: The matter of expertise is the problem with response (b). Particularly at the beginning of an

OD effort, the manager does not have the experience and knowledge required to decide what an appropriate OD intervention should be. The internal and/or external OD specialist has this expertise. The manager, then, should rely on this consultation for appropriate decision-making. He must be a part of the decision-making process, but he should not be the sole determiner of what the intervention is to be.

4. (b) The words "program," "laboratory," exercise," and "project" all have an *ad hoc* quality; they imply a one-time event. The term "process," on the other hand, conveys an ongoing activity. Organization Development should be seen as a continuing effort and not as an event which has a beginning and an end. Ideally, OD has no end.

5. (d) The Protestant ethic suggests "all work and no play," but OD advocates putting more fun into work. Socialism emphasizes collective ownership; OD does not. While OD is based on decentralizing power where applicable, and on other principles related to antiauthoritarianism, OD specialists do not necessarily advocate democratic methods (a system of elected representatives with an emphasis on social equality) for all organizations. Some of the values inherent in a truly democratic society (e.g., lack of suppression) are in the grain of OD. OD had its beginning in industrial organizations, but today it is used in government, church and other nonindustrial organizations.

   The underlying value system of OD stresses human dignity. Humanism asserts the dignity and worth of man and his capacity for self-realization. Advocates of OD emphasize that when management creates conditions whereby organizational members can more fully utilize their potential, the organization usually benefits and becomes more effective operationally. Moreover, OD accentuates a stronger integration of organizational members' needs with the organization's mission.

6. (c) T Group is a particular type of the more general form of education known as experience-based learning or the laboratory method of learning. Organization Development is a subpart of applied behavioral science in the same way that experience-based learning and clinical psychology are subparts.

7. (a) All of these organizations have been involved in Organization Development. The one with the longest history, however, is TRW Systems, with almost 10 years of OD activity.

8. (c) Carnegie Institute has courses in organization behavior and in management and thus touches on Organization Development indirectly. The other four institutions, however, have more active programs in organization behavior in their respective business or management schools; all four have a definite "OD flavor" to their learning objectives. If one wanted to get an advanced degree that would be heavily focused in Organization Development, he or she might apply to the Graduate School of Business Administration at UCLA, or the Sloan School of Management at MIT, or the Department of Organization Behavior at Case Western Reserve, or the Whittmore School of Business and Economics at the University of New Hampshire.
9. (d) There are at least three organizations in the United States which have as their name "Organization Development." One is the OD Network (not a formal part of but coordinated by the NTL Institute for Applied Behavioral Science) which has a membership of approximately 1300. Another is the OD Division of the American Society for Training and Development. This division has over 1000 members. A third organization is the OD Division of the Academy of Management. This division has over 100 members. There is some overlap of membership across these organizations, but the total number of individuals is certainly more than 2000 and is rapidly approaching 2500.
10. (d) Herb Shepard, Edgar Schein, Robert Blake, and Richard Beckhard have written in the field of Organization Development and are considered practitioners. While Peter Drucker has written prolifically in the fields of organization behavior and management, he has not written specifically in the field of Organization Development and is not seen as an OD practitioner. This is not to say that Drucker's work has nothing to do with OD. On the contrary, his pioneering work in Management By Objectives, for example, has considerable overlap and relevance to OD.
11. (e) Although some of Rogers' recent work has been concerned with organizations, his approach focuses primarily on the individual. The work of the other four men has considered individual behavior, but their primary thrust has been toward the group and the organization.

    Kurt Lewin developed a social psychological theory of human behavior and focused his research and theory accordingly. Douglas McGregor studied individual motivation and reward but his strategy for change emphasized the modification of organizational "systems"—the reward system, managerial practices, etc. Even though Elton Mayo's work helped to set off the "human relations" approach—an individual strategy of change—his research and theorizing was based on the study of formal organization in industry. His focus has been on the social system created when a small group of people work together. Fritz Roethlisberger is noted, among other things, for his work, along with Homans and Dickson, at the Hawthorne Works of Western Electric. The principles which have been derived from this work are based on studies of small work groups in an industrial setting.

These four men believed that individual behavior is largely a consequence of social factors such as the interaction of two people in a group, dynamics of the group itself, etc. Rogers stresses that human behavior is a consequence of individual factors such as the person's mental health and degree of a certain trait (i.e., empathy). This contrast is oversimplified, but the foundations of Organization Development are based more on the work of Lewin, McGregor, Mayo, and Roethlisberger than on that of Rogers.

12. (c) In Blake and Mouton's approach to OD, the 9,9 style of management is a team approach and is highly collaborative in nature. Likert's System 4 could be described similarly.

13. (e) The concept of differentiation-integration is the principle thesis of Lawrence and Lorsch. This principle is directly concerned with organizational structural change, particularly in terms of how effectively the organization's structure fits or matches the environmental demands (e.g., consumer market) placed on the system. While the other theorists/practitioners mentioned may become involved in structural change activities, it is not a mainstay of their respective approaches.

14. (a) While Blake and Mouton's approach to OD does not rule out surfacing and managing conflict, it is not listed as one of the steps in their six-phase outline.

15. (b) This is the name of one of Chris Argyris' books (Dorsey Press, 1962). In the field of Organization Development, Argyris is most closely associated with the area of interpersonal competence. It is his opinion that organizational effectiveness will never be fully achieved without interpersonal competence on the part of the managers within the organization.

16. (a) This item was taken directly from Rensis Likert's *Profile of Organizational Characteristics.* This questionnaire is a diagnostic

instrument explained by Likert in his book, *The Human Organization: Its Management and Value* (McGraw-Hill, 1967). The instrument provides a profile of an organization as perceived by its members, according to Likert's four "systems" of management —a team or group approach to management (a), consultative strategy (b), a benevolent approach (c), and an autocratic strategy (d).

17. (a) If you have read the Addison-Wesley series on OD, this item was probably easy for you. One of the books in the series, *Process Consultation,* was written by Edgar Schein. Another book in the series is Richard Walton's *Interpersonal Peacemaking: Confrontations and Third-Party Consultation.*

18. (d) The periodical *Psychology Today* has had some articles that have been related to organization behavior, but so far there has not been a paper focused exclusively on Organization Development.

19. (d) Force Field Analysis is a fairly simple procedure for determining what factors, or forces, seem to be contributing to a problem situation. The technique involves identifying the forces which appear to be moving a problem toward change and those which are providing a resistance to change. By examining in depth the resistant forces, one can frequently gain insight into what factors (forces) can be modified in ways that allow positive change to occur.

20. (a) Job enrichment as a potential technology of OD is based on Herzberg's theory of work motivation. Behavior modification as a technique and process of change is based on B. F. Skinner's theory of positive reinforcement. The only publication to date of behavior modification being applied to organizational change is the article, "At Emery Air Freight: Positive Reinforcement Boosts Performance," *Organizational Dynamics,* Winter, 1973, pp. 41–50.

21. (e) The OD consultant may at times use systems analysis and improvement. He should not only understand the sociotechnical approach to organization change, but apply it. The OD consultant is, in a sense, a social intervener when he works with an organization. But action research more adequately describes the OD consultant's approach to organization change. In brief, the OD consultant collects data (research), reports the data back to the client, and helps the client plan and take steps (action) of organizational improvement based on the data. As action is taken, the consultant collects further data on the consequences, feeds this

information back into the client system, helps the client to take further corrective action, etc. It is a continuous cycle.

22. (e) The first thing which must be clarified is "Who is the client?" In this situation, the assumption is that the client is the team—leader and members. Since part of the client system was eliminated, the consultant no longer has a defined client. With no client, my choice would be to withdraw from the situation until the client system was clarified. A team-building effort would leave a lot to be desired with a "lame duck" leader. Alternative (b) is attractive, and I may wish to take that kind of action, but it clearly has a lower priority than (e). Alternative (c) is inappropriate. First, it represents only part of the client system, and second, a work group without a leader is not an effective team. Reinstatement or relocation action is a management decision, not a consultant one.
23. (e) An inherent part of MBO is that a boss provides an opportunity for each of his subordinates to set objectives for himself, objectives which he thinks they can realistically reach. An underlying value of MBO is to provide more self-direction for organizational members.
24. (b) Organization Mirror is a design for a meeting which allows an organizational unit, such as the personnel department, to collect feedback from a number of pertinent units to which it relates (for example, manufacturing, marketing, and accounting). The purpose of the meeting is for the other units to provide helpful feedback to personnel so that they can improve their working relationships. For a description of this technique, see the book by Fordyce and Weil.
25. (c) This question was derived from Frank Friedlander's research in which he found that while (a), (b), (d), and (e) were statistically reliable outcomes, trust was *not* increased. Even though many people report that trust does increase as a result of this kind of intervention, Friedlander's study did not substantiate it. From a research viewpoint, the question to be raised is whether Friedlander's results can be replicated. (The main purpose of including this last question is to stimulate you to read the research theory and case studies in the field!)

Give yourself 4 points for each correct answer. If you scored less than 72, well, I guess it's your opinion against mine. If you scored more than 72, don't rush out and sell your OD books. The test just covered some of the basics, you know. W.W.B.

3

PLANNED ORGANIZATIONAL CHANGE

In Chapter 1 we tried to give you some sense of the need for an Organization Development approach to managing change in your organization. In Chapter 2 we defined what we meant by OD, gave you a brief history, and tried to prepare you for thinking about what approach you would use in bringing about change in your organization.

This chapter is designed to give you specific information about what OD is and how an OD strategy of change may work more favorably for you than other strategies. The conclusion of this chapter should help you make a decision to use or not to use an OD strategy for organizational change.

STRATEGIES FOR CHANGE

Dr. Kurt E. Olmosk identifies eight basic strategies of change which managers can use. Briefly these are described as follows:*

1. *Political Strategy:* This is a strategy that is based on understanding the power structure that people must deal with in the organization. This power structure usually includes not only the formal, recognized leaders, but also the informal leaders. Once powerful people have been identified, the strategy is to work closely with them to bring about the change.
2. *Economic Strategy:* Emphasis in this approach is on acquiring or, at least, having influence over all forms of material goals. For instance, if you hold the budget strings in your hand, then you have power over people by virtue of saying yes or no to the use of the budget.
3. *Academic Strategy:* This assumes that people are rational. If you present enough facts to the people, people will make the change required. In other words, you try to bring about change based on the rational approach to change, convincing people by the facts themselves.
4. *Engineering Strategy:* Here we bring about change in individual behavior by dealing directly with people. The assumption seems to be, if the environment or surrounding changes enough, people

* Olmosk, K. E., in *The 1972 Annual Handbook for Group Facilitators*, J. W. Pfeiffer and J. E. Jones (Eds.), (La Jolla, Cal.: University Associates, 1972), p. 163. Reprinted by permission.

will change also. In other words, if you would like to bring about a change in someone, you change the environment in which he or she lives. For instance, if you wish to have someone wear a coat, you reduce the temperature in his or her room. Or, to put it in more practical terms, if you wish to increase the speed at which people are working, you speed up the machine.

5. *Military Strategy:* This approach to change is based on the physical force which some leaders hold. They are able to use a military or hereditarian approach on other people. Or in other terms, you use the revolutionary approach, or violence, to force people to change, instead of persuading them.

6. *Confrontation Strategy:* In this approach, change is based on the assumption that if you can mobilize enough anger and enough people, and force them to look at the problems around them, the required changes will be made. The whole point is to make people so uncomfortable that they have no choice but to move in the direction that you'd like them to move, playing primarily on their emotions.

7. *Applied Behavioral Science Model:* In this approach we apply various types of change strategies. In general, it is a combination of the various approaches which we've already mentioned. This is a highly complex approach to change in that it requires a considerable amount of skill to be able to identify the variables which are involved in the change strategy. It usually requires the assistance of a behavioral scientist.

8. *Fellowship Strategy:* In simple terms the fellowship strategy, which is the strategy used by most OD professionals, goes something like this. If we have good interpersonal relationships, the problems will be minor. If we can concentrate on our process—the way in which we work together—at least as much as we do on getting the job accomplished, we would do a better job. I am not certain whether I would personally agree with the use of the words "fellowship strategy" as opposed to something like "participative strategy"; however, I believe that Kurt Olmosk very clearly makes the point that most OD professionals use this model. It emphasizes a number of things: people need to be involved in what they are doing or the things that are going on around them; they must be accepted into membership and not turned away; decision-making must be jointly shared; facts and information as well as feelings and opinions need to get out on the table; argu-

ments may be few but when they do occur they need to be dealt with directly.

An OD approach to change, although not limited to any one of the above strategies, tends to emphasize the fellowship strategy and the participative strategy. The reason for this is the underlying assumption that human beings are basically good and competent and that, given the opportunity to participate and join in the activities which they are involved in, they will direct their energies in a positive way. In our discussion we will not limit ourselves to just one strategy. We will, however, tend to emphasize the fellowship strategy. The other options are still open to managers and should be carefully considered in terms of the results which they may produce.

AN OVERVIEW OF THE OD APPROACH TO CHANGE

One of the ways in which we can describe what happens in OD is to be clear about the objectives we are attempting to accomplish, what we are assuming to be desirable organizational goals, and the processes which need to be looked at in order to bring about the change which we are attempting to make. The schematic diagram in Fig. 3.1 helps to explain this.

We assume that the desired goals listed in Fig. 3.1 are common to most organizations and that the OD objectives of developing an "adaptable and relevant" organization are also acceptable to most managers. In its simplest form OD focuses on organizational processes with the object being to improve so that organization and individual goals are more readily attainable.

J. Jennings Partin (1973) identifies three characteristics of OD important to a manager. First, he points out that the target for change is basically the total organization or a large unit as opposed to an individual. Second, the goal for any OD effort should be for improvement in organization effectiveness or performance. Third, he indicates that the changes which are being made by managers need to be based on theoretical conceptual behavioral science models and information as opposed to seat-of-the-pants approaches. The relationship of management practices to how individuals feel in an organization, plus their behavior and relationship to outcomes, are really the critical issues. Partin suggests that OD is not a short-term strategy but rather a long-

Fig. 3.1 OD approaches to change

Desired Organizational Goals	Objectives of OD	Organizational Processes Involved
Work is managed against goals. Organization structure is developed out of function. Decisions are made near source of information (authority of knowledge as well as role). Communications are undistorted. There is high collaboration and low competition. Conflict which is inevitable is managed. A feeling of ownership of change efforts. Teams are the basic unit of work. There are built-in, continuous improvement mechanisms.	To develop a viable organization that is highly adaptable and relevant to: 1. A changing environment 2. Changing needs and goals of members	Decision-making and problem-solving Planning and goal-setting Communications Leadership and authority Cultural norms and values Intergroup relations Member values and functions

term strategy which may last several years. As a matter of fact, it may be an ongoing and continuous process within an organization.

The underlying notion of OD is by no means a simple, uncomplicated practice or program which a manager can put into effect without careful thought. In fact, a complex strategy for change has a much higher degree of potential payoff than does a basic short-range strategy such as using power or political influence on an individual or a group of individuals. We hope you will realize that the purpose behind an OD strategy or approach to change is a lasting viability as opposed to a short-term gain.

We need to be clear at this point that we are not attempting to make a manager into a social scientist or into a full-fledged OD professional. Our purpose in writing this is to help managers understand the concept of OD. We believe it would be foolhardy to think, after having read this book, that a manager would feel fully qualified and feel confortable to handle all types of OD interventions.

ESSENTIAL CONDITIONS FOR THE SUCCESS OF AN OD EFFORT

Wendell L. French (1973) described a number of conditions which he feels are essential to deriving optimal success in an organizational development effort. They are as follows:

1. Perceptions of organizational problems by key people, and perceptions of the relevance of the behavioral sciences in solving these problems.
2. The introduction into the system of a behavioral scientist-consultant.
3. Initial top-level involvement, or at least support from a higher echelon with subsequent top-management involvement.
4. The operationalizing of the action research model.
5. Early successes, with expansion of the effort stemming from these successes.
6. An open, educational philosophy about the theory and the technology of OD.
7. Acknowledgment of the congruency between OD and many previous effective management practices.
8. Involvement of personnel and industrial people and congruency with personnel policy and practice.
9. Development of internal OD resources.
10. Effective management of the OD processes.
11. Monitoring the process and the measuring of results.

Many of the points French makes about the conditions which are necessary for the success of OD will be covered in the remaining sections of this manual. We do not believe that all of these conditions are necessary before embarking on an OD program, but certainly some are worthy of consideration as you attempt to look at your organization.

One large corporation identified five essential conditions which *must* be met for an OD effort to be successful (General Motors, 1974). They are as follows:

1. OD is essentially a *line* function; therefore, it *must* respond directly to important *business* problems.
2. OD *must* be based on a comprehensive *theory* which guides the solving of those problems.

3. OD *must* be an extension of the *chief executive officer.*
4. OD *must* involve the authentic use of *power* by all managers in the organization.
5. OD *must* be supported by a *staff* competent to provide technical and "participative" assistance.

J. A. Foltz of H. J. Heinz Company stated that there are two basic requisites for effective OD effort in his company: (1) four organizational concepts, and (2) the chief executive officer fusing these four concepts together.

The four concepts (shown in Fig. 3.2) are:

1. A CEO who recognizes that
   a) His primary accountability is profit, but
   b) His primary responsibility is OD—the chief means for attaining profit.
2. A special VP exclusively concerned with OD and clearly an extension of the officer of the CEO.
3. An external professional, trained in the behavioral sciences, who
   a) facilitates the internal management's discharge of *their* primary OD accountabilities, and

Fig. 3.2 Relationship of OD concepts

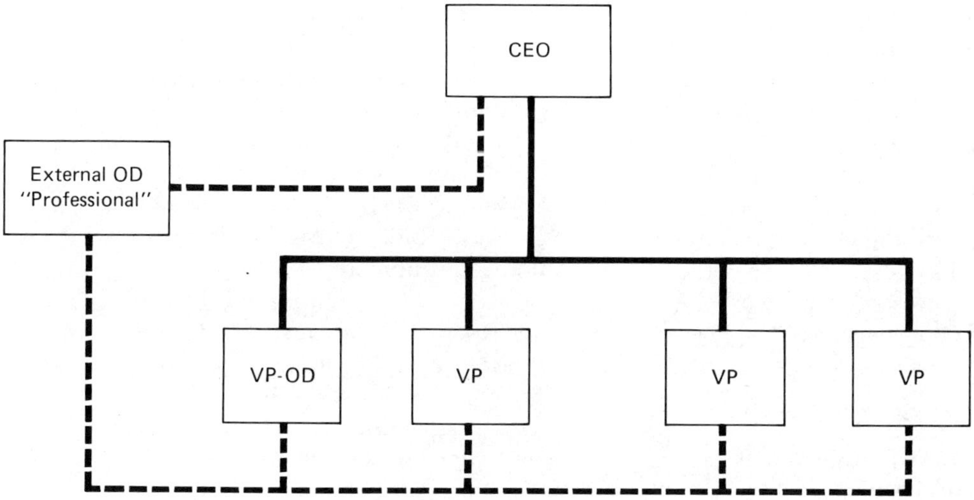

b) services as a "source of reality."

4. A group of "functional" managers (in marketing, finance, production, distribution, business development*) who:
   a) are functionally knowledgeable,
   b) are managerially competent,
   c) have a sense of urgency, and
   d) have clear notions of the interrelationships of their accountabilities.

It seems clear that for OD to work in an organization the *line* manager must be involved, it must have top support, it must be based on sound theories and principles, and it most have a human or authentic quality instead of displaying simply a raw use of power. One other condition seems to be apparent: There must be some professionally based knowledge available to the organization either internally or externally (external OD consultant).

IS OD JUST ANOTHER FAD?

Is OD just another passing fad for which managers may wish to get on the bandwagon, or is it a fundamentally new approach to organizational change? Probably this question still remains to be answered. However, as a study by the National Industrial Conference Board in 1973 has pointed out, it seems quite clear that "As a process of systematic change, it becomes institutionalized as a problem-centered and results-oriented way of life." The Conference Board is suggesting that it is not a fad but an approach which it appears will be with us into the future. There are some examples, however, and marked tendencies on the part of some proponents of OD to become wrapped up in the latest techniques of OD interventions instead of looking at the basic strategy of Organization Development. There are many consultants, professors, and organizational behavioral specialists who have been associated with the OD approach who are making it look like a "flash in the pan." The real test of whether Organization Development is a lasting and viable concept, we believe, will come when a financial crunch hits. If OD specialists, departments and activities do not succumb to the economic woes which all organizations face at one time or another,

---

* And related functions such as personnel, employee communications, public relations and all employee and office services.

then OD will likely represent a permanent activity for managers and organizations to embrace.

OBJECTIVES OF OD

We touched on the objectives of a typical OD program earlier as we laid out an overview of it. Although the objectives of any OD effort may vary according to the situation an organization is facing, its problems, and the general goals it's attempting to achieve, we believe that there are several major goal orientations which Organization Development, out of necessity, must make. They are as follows:

1. To increase the basic organizational effectiveness (performance) and to make the organization a more acceptable place for people to work.
2. To build trust among individuals and groups throughout the organization.
3. To create an open, problem-solving climate where problems are confronted and differences are clarified both for the in group and in-between groups.
4. To locate decision-making and problem-solving responsibility as close to the information sources and relevant sources of data as possible.
5. To find ways to increase the sense of ownership or the feeling of belonging that people need to experience in their organizations.
6. To move toward a more participative approach to managing between individuals and groups within an organization; to strive for a cooperative approach as opposed to a competitive approach.
7. To increase the sensitivity of people in an organization to the processes underlying the ability that they have to perform in the organization; at least to focus 50% of one's effort on the process of the organization as opposed to the task of the organization; the rationale for this is that without awareness of the process the task gets muddied up and often is not accomplished, whereas by paying attention to the process the task will be accomplished much more readily.

One national organization, Saga Food, has an extensive Organization Development program and they are generally cited as having a successful OD effort. Their OD objectives are:

1. To enable Saga people to be exposed to, and acquire, the human relations skills needed to make them maximally effective human beings by fulfilling their highest personal goals and objectives in every situation while meeting the needs of all concerned.
2. To help individuals to become truly aware of themselves in every portion of their being at all times.
3. To assist people in gaining knowledge and insight about the impact of their behavior—whatever it is—at any given moment.
4. To create a climate of emotional security so that individuals can talk about how they feel. Thus, feeling can be on top of the table where they can be dealt with as such, rather than hidden forces that warp logic and distort judgments.
5. To prompt individuals to govern their own behavior so that it becomes a conscious force for achieving goals, not an ungovernable force which results in actions spurred by emotions alone.
6. To condition participants to be fully aware of how people behave, function and feel, so that they can have a better understanding of how to best use their own skills in directing their behavior and in relating to others.
7. To expand each person's understanding of the realities, forces and dynamics in every situation so that he or she can consciously apply the kind of behavior that will cause the situation to improve.
8. To guide each person in formulating goals and objectives for every situation or relationship of which he or she is a part.
9. To discourage individuals from viewing OD as "soft-style management," and to encourage directness and effectiveness in dealing with tough situations. The real OD behavior is that which is fully congruent with the situation at hand.
10. To provide Saga managers and the Saga systems with methods to achieve the comprehensive nature of OD which, in reality, should be called the "Saga Way of Management."

The objectives for your own OD program need to be established by you to fit your needs; however we believe they should include the basic objective of improving the human organization.

WHAT OD CAN'T DO

There are some strong arguments for what OD can do, but there are also some counterarguments relative to what OD can't do. Organization Development is not a panacea for all problems in an organization.

Organization Development cannot:

1. Create a 100% harmonious organization in which all people work together in a completely collaborative and supportive way.
2. Make an organization completely effective and efficient. Organization Development is an approach which, when considered with other complex variables in the organization, has a high probability of helping the organization become more effective.
3. Be readily measured. Therefore it is difficult to support the need for—or substantiate the value of—OD to top management. It relies upon the intuitive values to be gained from such an approach.
4. Change a failing organization into a successful organization overnight. Organization Development is basically a change strategy in which you are attempting to change the social structures and processes within an organization to make it a more viable organization.

FACTORS THAT MAKE FOR A SUCCESSFUL OD EFFORT

The principal factors which will determine whether an OD effort is successful or a failure in your organization seem to be summarized as follows:

1. There must be active support and involvement from top management.
2. Members of the organization must change their thoughts and feelings as a result of the OD efforts.
3. It is not a training strategy and therefore must be thought of as basically an approach which is aimed at changing the way in which people work together.
4. You are attempting to change the climate of the organization as well as the social processes within the organization.
5. The investment of time at the front end or beginning of such an OD effort will not realize a payoff until sometime well into the future.
6. There is no one approach to organizational change which is best, but the approach using what knowledge we have about management sciences today seems to be the best.
7. Organization development programs must not be thought of as a new "package" program being brought into the organization to solve its problems. We refer here to the way in which many

programs get introduced, such as Management By Objectives. Generally, it is most successful where it is thought of as being a well-timed or subtle approach to organizational change.

ANALYZING YOUR OWN ORGANIZATION

This section has suggested a number of ways to think about OD and how it might work for you. In the remainder of this section we would like you to analyze your own organization and to test the viability of applying OD to your organization. We suggest you complete the following "self analysis" for your organization.

I. What are the most common change strategies used in your organization? Apply a percent distribution by taking 10 points and distributing them among the following change strategies according to their application in your organization. (Refer to the first section of this chapter: Strategies for Change.)

_____ Political strategy
_____ Economic strategy
_____ Academic strategy
_____ Engineering strategy
_____ Military strategy
_____ Confrontation strategy
_____ Applied behavioral science model
_____ Fellowship strategy
_____ Other strategy not listed above ____________
____

Which strategy listed above is most practiced in your organization —and why?

____
____
____
____
____
____

II. Check those of the following conditions essential to successful OD that are present in your organization.

Perceptions of organizational problems by key people, and perceptions of the relevance of the behavioral sciences to solving these problems.

The introduction into the system of a behavioral scientist-consultant. ______

Initial top-level involvement, or at least support from a higher echelon with subsequent top-management involvement. ______

The operationalizing of the action research model. ______

Early successes, with expansion of the effort stemming from these successes. ______

An open, educational philosophy about the theory and the technology of OD. ______

Acknowledgment of the congruency between OD and many previous effective management practices. ______

Involvement of personnel and industrial people and congruency with personnel policy and practice. ______

Development of internal OD resources. ______

Effective management of the OD processes. ______

Monitoring the process and the measuring of results. ______

III. Check those of the following objectives for OD that apply to the needs of your organization. ______

To increase the basic organizational effectiveness (performance) and to make the organization a more acceptable place for people to work. ______

To build trust among individuals and groups throughout the organization. ______

To create an open, problem-solving climate in which problems are confronted and differences are clarified both for the in group and in-between groups. ______

To locate decision-making and problem-solving responsibility as close to the information sources and relevant sources of data as possible. ______

To find ways to increase the sense of ownership or the feeling of belonging that people need to experience in their organizations. ______

To move toward a more participative approach to managing between individuals and groups within an organization; to strive for a cooperative approach instead of a competitive approach. ______

To increase the sensitivity of people in an organization to the processes underlying the ability that they have to perform in the organization; to focus at least 50% of one's effort on the process of the organization as opposed to the task of the organization. The rationale for this is that without awareness of the process the task gets muddied up, many times not accomplished; if people pay attention to the process, the task will be accomplished much more readily.

The preceding analysis should provide you with a summary of the status of your organization and its readiness for OD. If, for example, you find that the military strategy for change is most pronounced in your organization, this suggests that you will probably have a more difficult time introducing other OD-oriented strategies. On the other hand, if the conditions are right for OD, perhaps such conditions would encourage acceptance of an OD effort. After you have analyzed your data, write a summary statement below which describes the readiness of your organization for an OD program.

4

STEPS IN THE ORGANIZATION DEVELOPMENT PROCESS

In the preceding chapter we discussed the nature of planned organizational change and laid out a basic overview of the OD process and the approaches which are used. We talked about what OD can and cannot do for you and raised the question about whether Organization Development can be useful and bring about systematic change in your organization.

The purpose of this chapter is to examine the actual steps involved in conducting an OD "intervention." Here we would like to walk you through the basic steps of the OD process and pay particular attention to how you design an Organization Development intervention for your own organization.

SOME BASIC IDEAS

One of the important points you need to know about the intervention or the steps involved in the OD process is the great reliance placed on the organization to solve its own problems. This is much different from other types of research and organizational analysis usually conducted in organizations. The organization itself must collect data about its behavior and how it is working, make decisions relative to what the data suggest, and then implement action steps to solve its own problems. In the jargon of the Organization Development field, this is called "action research." Essentially, it involves the following basic steps:

1. Recognition of the problem.
2. Collecting information and data about the problem.
3. Analyzing the problem and the alternatives to solving it.
4. Actually designing solution objectives and implementation steps.
5. Implementing the change.

These various steps look similar to the typical steps involved in most technical or social research. The basic distinction is that instead of having data collected by an outside, third party, the organization collects the data itself, in its own self-interest. The organization also interprets the information and designs the actual steps to be taken for bringing about change. How this works in reality is that a third party helps design the data collection approach, but the actual data collection is done with full knowledge of the organization and all of those involved. Interpretation is not done by one individual, but by the organization as a whole.

A second point is the recognition that the necessary changes involve the total organization and usually are aimed at improving the organization's effectiveness and, in particular, profitability. The various management processes and activities which would be examined in an OD process include:

1. Organization structure
2. Job definition
3. Employee compensation
4. Decision-making
5. Planning of activities
6. Administration of policies, procedures, and practices
7. Evaluation of individual and organizational performance
8. Communication of information
9. Development of people
10. Learning processes within the organization

The OD approach does not force you to merely look at how people work together. It also looks at all related activities.

Another important thing to note is that there are various levels within the organization which may become involved in the OD process. These levels largely determine the kind of approach used in solving the problem. The levels range from individuals to teams to intergroups to the total organization.

The purpose of the intervention at each of these levels would be as follows:

1. At the *individual level* we would attempt to improve personal competency.
2. At the team level we would improve effectiveness of the team.
3. At the intergroup level we would improve working relationships between teams.
4. At the total organizational level we want to get a better sense of direction for the organization and the necessary supporting structures to make it possible for the organization to move in the direction it wants to go.

Typical examples of OD activities (technology) which are frequently used at these various levels involve:

Individual level: Life planning, individual needs, and training needs.

Team level: *Work procedures*—task accomplishment, decision-making, and agenda. *Interpersonal relations*—feelings and attitudes.

Intergroup level: Mutual understanding, cooperation, reduced disfunctional competition, and communications.

Total organization level: Planning, purpose, objectives, goals, organizational flexibility, form-follows-function, and communications.

Since the OD approach is applicable to all levels and to various types of problems, the type of strategy which you design to solve the problem at these various levels obviously differs.

MODELS FOR ORGANIZATION CHANGE

In a report written in 1973, Charles J. Margerison lists a number of phases which he sees an organization going through in order to bring about organizational change. They are:

1. Comparing present behavior of the organization with future needs of the organization.
2. Establishing objectives and purposes for change.
3. Assessing the nature of the problem by getting data from the people involved with the change.
4. Presenting this information to those involved with the change as data to be considered and used in generating alternative courses of action.
5. Establishing meetings to evaluate alternatives and planning decisions.
6. Implementing the solutions.
7. Reviewing and establishing an adaptive system of change.

As Margerison points out, "This may seem a bit formal and forbidding." It is, however, little more than what actually happens in a somewhat haphazard way in most change efforts in an organization. Most organizations actually go through these various steps but probably not consciously. The purpose of an OD strategy is to look at the steps more systematically and to plan them out in a more logical and more deliberate way.

Another way to view the Organization Development process was described in The Conference Board Report (1973), which laid out a model for organization development as shown in Fig. 4.1. The basic nature of this model involves self-examination by the organization to see how it is performing and what problems it's creating for itself. The second step is the development of a strategy for change, that is, deciding what steps, approaches and actions will be taken to bring about the change. The intervention portion of the model involves the action-change process itself.

Fig. 4.1 A model for OD (From *Organization Development: A Reconnaissance,* National Industrial Conference Board, 1973. Used by permission.)

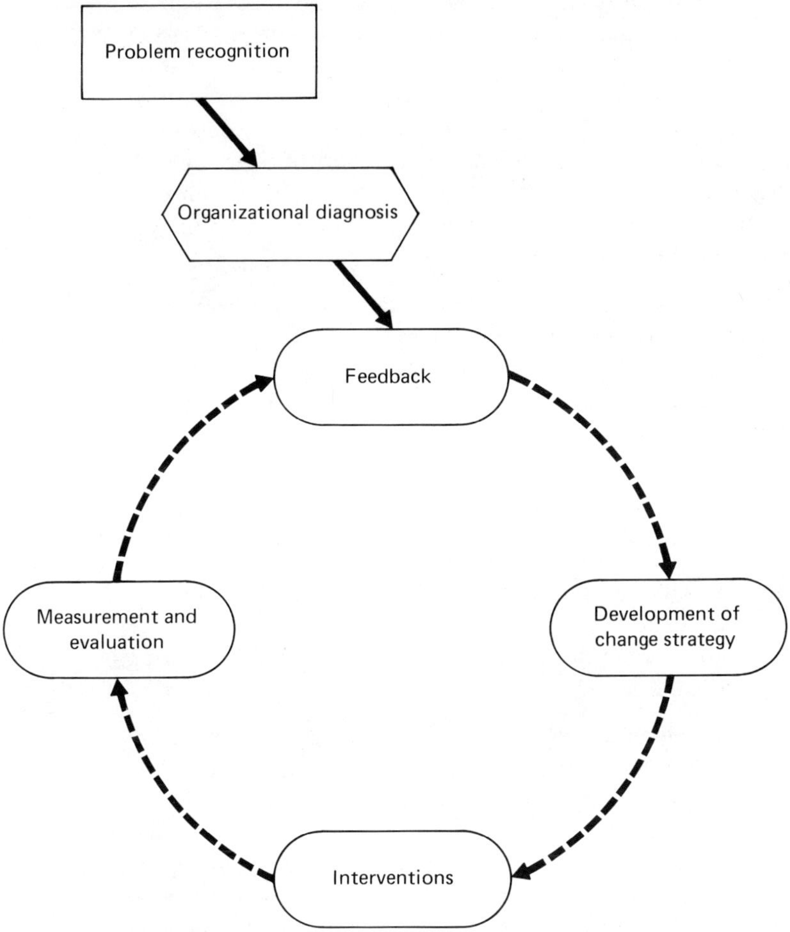

In our terms we define the intervention as the total process, including the feedback development of the change strategy, the actual intervention, and the measurement and evaluation phase. As will be explained later, the intervention starts where data are collected. Finally, the measuring and evaluation phases involve actually measuring the progress which is being made toward the achievement of the change objectives established by the organization. This is an essential part of the OD process oftentimes overlooked by managers when they are dealing with organizational changes involving human beings.

We now want to discuss systematically the way we see a manager implementing a change strategy within his or her organization. This takes into consideration those variables and factors which are most significant and which are most likely to cause problems in implementing the change. Therefore, we ask you to think of yourself as a third party to your organization (an outsider looking in). Step back from your position as a manager and think about how you would design an intervention for changing your organization if you were an outside consultant brought in to help bring about the change. Cast yourself in the role of a consultant to your organization; we think that this will help you better understand the problems involved.

We intend here to describe a framework for designing an OD intervention strategy. For our purpose we define an intervention as any move into an organization, group, or between individuals with the objective of helping the organization, group, or individuals to change the way they work together to achieve more effective performance.

An intervention into an organization creates a disruption which, we hope, results in improved functioning of the organization. Careful planning of such an intervention is incumbent on the manager.

If you are concerned with designing an intervention strategy for your organization, you should recognize that several different substrategies may be required to cover each of the following stages in the consulting process as shown in Fig. 4.2.

The strategy used at the preentry stage may be quite different from the strategy used during the design of actual intervention stage. The reason for this is obvious; what you know about the client and his or her organization at the preentry point is often different from what you know about it at the design-of-intervention stage. By the second stage you have increased your data bank of knowledge and, consequently, have a clearer grasp of the nature of the organization and the correct strategy to use. It is important to be aware that your strategies will be changing from one stage to the next and that what works in one stage may not work in another. The strategy that is designed around limited data may, in fact, have to be adjusted or discarded at the next stage as additional data are gathered.

NATURE OF AN INTERVENTION STRATEGY

An intervention strategy can be characterized in at least four different ways:

Fig. 4.2 Steps in the OD process

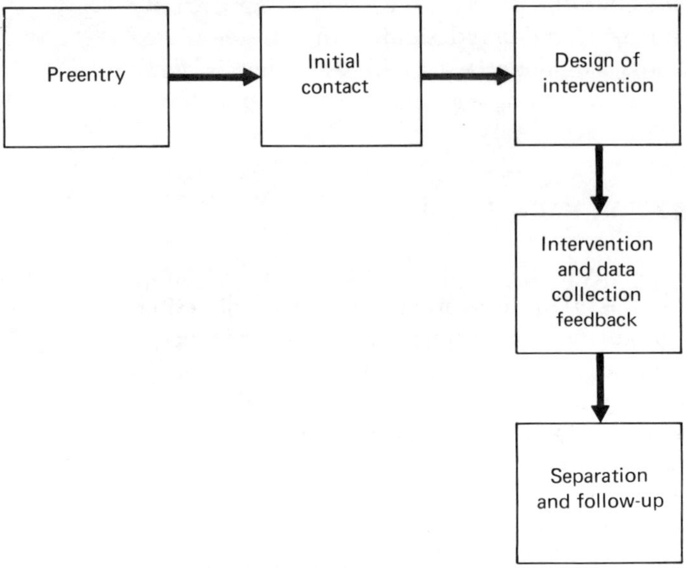

1. It is a plan for conducting the intervention itself; that is, it lays out a set of steps and actions which will be followed by the process consultant on the basis of his or her knowledge of the organization at any particular time.
2. An intervention strategy is necessarily flexible and adaptable to the changing organizational situation. A strategy which is inflexible will quite likely yield no improvement. For example, pushing for a change in procedures when members of the organization see no need for the change may increase resistance, resulting in less cooperation, poor performance, etc.
3. In all cases the strategy designed to meet a specific situation must have alternate approaches built into it. The purpose is to meet any situation which may present itself. For example, the process consultant makes a decision to collect data around a certain issue or problem, and, at the next meeting, the client suddenly decides to take over the discussion for another purpose. The process consultant is then required to use an alternative strategy to meet the changing situation.
4. An intervention strategy is usually designed within a general framework until actual contact with the client is made. That is, the consultant could go into the client organization with a general

set (strategy) in mind, but with no fixed notion of how to approach the client. This gives the process consultant an opportunity to get the "lay of the land" before designing the strategy. The strategy, in other words, could be "wait and see" what is going on in the organization or in the client's mind.

DESIGNING STRATEGIES FOR EACH STAGE

One way to view an OD strategy is to consider it as the overall strategy used with a client to guide the OD intervention in a general direction. Such a general strategy might be, for example, to always encourage the elements of the organization to unload information relative to where they are at a particular moment so that each step in the OD process might start off with a data collecting process. Another overall strategy might be to always approach an organization with the understanding that the first step in the intervention is to conduct a personal sharing session; to help people get in touch with their feelings and ideas and be willing to share these with others. Whatever the overall strategy is, it is clear that there is a series of substrategies associated with it. These substrategies can be identified in terms of the consulting stages listed above.

We will briefly discuss each of the stages in terms of the type of questions which the process consultant should be asking himself or herself while designing substrategies for each stage (refer to Fig. 4.2).

1. *Preentry stage*—Typical questions that need to be answered are:

   a) Who is the client (organization, unit, department, people)? What are the client's products, services? Functions? Who is the primary leadership person and what is he or she like? How large is the organization? What is the general character of the organization? How did you get involved? What is your relationship, etc.?

   b) What are your theories about the organization in terms of what you saw prior to preentry? Being aware of your theories and basic bias toward the organization is essential if you expect to be able to assist the organization to make the change it would like to make.

   c) How do you expect the client to behave once you make initial contact?

d) What will you do if your expectations are not lived up to or for some reason you have completely misjudged the organization? What will the organization do if its expectations are not met?

2. *Initial-contact stage*—This particular stage involves preparation for and entry into the organization. Typical questions that need to be raised here are as follows:

   a) What are the objectives of the intervention and what criteria will be used to measure the results (see the next section: Criteria for Measuring a Successful Intervention)?

   b) How will you conduct the initial meeting?

   c) How much time should you use to solve the problem?

   d) What will the agenda be and will it be set?

   e) What additional data do you need about the organization and its problems?

   f) What will you do if there is a basic incongruity between the intervention strategy which you have designed and the organization's needs?

   g) What will you do in terms of checking your relationship with the organization to see if you are making progress toward a binding contract to work for the organization?

   h) What are the restraining and moving forces in the organization?

3. *Design of intervention*—The design and actual intervention which will be used in the organization must answer these three questions:

   a) What are the key variables in the relationship which will determine success or failure of the intervention? For example, perhaps those involved in the change can not accept a change which is inconsistent with their values; therefore, knowledge of what people believe in is essential.

   b) What behavioral theories and concepts can you use in understanding the relationship and how will these theories be used to help the organization?

   c) What types of approaches can you use to determine the basic character of the organization (climate, health, and so forth—see Chapter 5) and what techniques—such as team building, cousins-groups, mirroring, fish-bowling (see Chapter 9)—should be used to help the organization solve its problems? (See Appendix I for list of resources for use in OD intervention.)

4. *Intervention and data-collection feedback*—At the data-collection stage there are three primary questions that need to be answered:

   a) What data-collection techniques will be used to find out about the organization? Should you use a questionnaire approach, interviews, or sensing meetings (group meetings designed to find out what's going on)?

   b) What should the timing be? How long should the process consultant be engaged in the actual process of data collection? How should this be scheduled? On site or off site? What should the various logistics be, including how to notify employees that the process consultant will be making this intervention? What role should the employees play in the data-collection process, etc.?

   c) What feedback approaches will be used? Will it be a simple report to the organization, will it be a feedback session with top management, or will it be a series of small meetings with all the employees of the organization? Just exactly how will the information be fed back to the organization?

In the feedback and change phase of your relationship the responsibility for change is primarily in the hands of the organization. You are *only* obligated to *help* the organization develop its own goals, strategies, and tactics. You can help the organization see itself and the way it is functioning. You can observe the kinds of things going on and note how this affects results and effectiveness, but you can't *make* it change. This is an important distinction. For example, the author was recently working with a group of hospital supervisors when the head of hospital maintenance (who was a somewhat outspoken but dedicated type) interrupted the group as they were processing data about the organization. He asked me, "Just what makes you think you can get us to change the way we are doing things around here?"

It was quite apparent that he was questioning the consulting relationship and what I could do to help. I finally told the group, "You probably can solve your own problems, if you put your minds to it. You have all the resources right here and now. The only thing I can do is help you look at yourself and perhaps facilitate some of the changes that you want to make." The question resolved itself later when the group accepted the responsibility for design and change by themselves. Several sessions later I left the organization, reasonably confident they would indeed solve their problems.

5. *Separation and follow-up*—Basic questions to be answered at this point in the design of an intervention strategy are:

a) What were the results of the intervention?

b) Were you helpful?

c) What does the organization expect of you in the future?

d) What can the organization tell you about the way you handled the relationship? This is very important if you want to be effective in an OD relationship. This provides you with the opportunity to collect data about your own behavior and the effect you have had on the organization.

ESSENTIALS IN DESIGNING AN EFFECTIVE OD INTERVENTION STRATEGY

There are a number of things that are critical to the design of an effective OD intervention strategy:

1. You must view your role as one involving careful planning and theorizing relative to the organization. This means investment of considerable time in planning out what your strategies will be.
2. You must be highly flexible (quick on your feet) in order to adapt your strategy to the situation at hand. If you are rigid and inflexible, you will find your overall strategy may not work.
3. An intervention strategy designed for a specific organization can be tested on others for its validity. In other words, it is a recommended step to try out your ideas on others to make sure your strategies are designed in a way which will be meaningful and useful to the organization.
4. You must be aware of the basic theories which you carry around in your head relative to individuals, groups of people and organizations. These theories oftentimes lead you to following a favorite set of strategies for all situations. The chances of this happening are obvious, but remember that one or two basic and proven approaches may not work in all situations. Just because it's comfortable for you doesn't mean it will work in all organizations.

CRITERIA FOR MEASURING A SUCCESSFUL INTERVENTION

Intervention into an organization and the associated strategies are difficult to measure but may be evaluated in terms of the following questions:

1. Does the organization feel that you helped them? Were they satisfied that their problems were resolved?
2. Do you feel you helped the organization? Did you come away with useful information about your own skills and about what you did to help the organization?
3. Did you, in the process of solving one problem, create another? (If you walk out of an organization having created additional problems or other types of problems for the organization, you could hardly call your intervention a success.)
4. Do members of the organization feel that you can help them in other ways? Will they want you back and would they like to use your skills in future problems they may have?
5. Does the organization have a new look or a new approach or a new feeling about how they can solve future problems? Do they seem to have a better grasp of different approaches to solving their problems?
6. Did the organization find out things about itself which were not known before and what kind of reaction did the organization have to this information? If it was a positive reaction and a feeling that they now have new grasps of their problems, then this is a sign that the process consultant was helpful to the organization.

We believe that if a manager follows this framework in looking at his or her organization, the chances of successfully implementing change will be increased substantially. These steps are not regarded as absolute and any manager who is following them should feel free to vary them depending on the circumstances being faced and the particular needs of the organization. They simply represent a set of steps which may be regarded as a broad framework for bringing about systematic organizational change.

As we have done in each of the preceding sections, we want the reader to experiment with OD. This, we believe, is the way you learn to use OD concepts and ideas to help you manage more effectively. We would like you to draw up a rough outline of an OD strategy designed to solve a specific problem in your own organization. Remember this is not a final operational design. It is a practice design to give you a feel for OD strategy planning.

Please Complete the Following Sections

I. Briefly define the specific problem (examples might be two groups not communicating well, or poor departmental meetings, etc.)

II. What levels of personnel are involved (individual, teams, intergroup, total organization).

III. Write a brief statement about each of the following intervention steps. (See questions in the section on Designing Strategies for Each Stage, earlier in this chapter.)

Preentry

Initial contact

Design of intervention

Intervention, data collection, and feedback

Separation and follow-up

____

____

____

IV. What specific things do you plan to do at each of the intervention stages?

Preentry (getting ready)

____

____

____

Initial contact (meetings with those involved to introduce idea)

____

____

____

Design of intervention (what will you do)

____

____

____

Actual data collection and feedback

____

____

____

Separation and follow-up

____

____

____

V. What problems do you anticipate in implementing your OD strategy?

____

____

____

____

As you go on through this book you may want to return to look at your strategy design. Later in the book we will ask you to complete a more detailed OD intervention design.

5

FACTORS AFFECTING NEED FOR CHANGE

The following conversation takes place in a typical organization among three men who have been asked to work together on a committee for the purpose of redesigning a performance-appraisal program.

John: It's good of you to come in this morning. Sorry to take so much of your time for this task. I know how some of you feel about this. As you know, J.C. asked us to take a look at our performance-appraisal system which we've had in operation now for about six years. What he wants us to do is to see if we can come up with an alternate system which will work better for us. Some of the problems that we've had, you know, are that the people are resisting using the system. We're not getting good reports back, people are generally opposed and we're hearing all kinds of complaints about it. I guess what I want to do to get started is to ask your viewpoints on the system and how it works.

Harry: Can I say something? You know I'm busy as hell and I really don't want to be here. So whatever you two guys want to do, it's alright with me. I'll really pitch in whatever the decision. I've gone around with this thing for three years now and I really don't care any more. So go ahead guys.

John: Well, I'd still like to get you involved though, Harry. I'd like to know how you feel about it. I know you have some definite thoughts and I don't want to miss the opportunity of hearing those from you.

Carl: In my opinion, we should start talking about why people have resisted what we've been doing so far. Try to develop some basis for any kind of revision we should go through.

John: I think Carl has a point—that we should take a serious look at this. Let's go back and find out what causes them to feel this way. I think this is a good place to start.

Harry: I think you are operating on the premise that something's wrong with the present system. I don't really see what's wrong with it.

John: Do I understand you correctly that you don't think that there is?

Harry: Here again, I really don't care, but it's working so what do we want to change it for?

Carl: I feel that we've gotten some resistance from the people involved in it because it's a fairly sterile kind of approach. It does seem to have worked fairly effectively in many ways but instead of getting us started on something it's sterile in the sense of building the individual and building the basis for understanding. It would seem to me that a good analysis of what we have would be the desirable thing to do and then build from there.

John: I can understand how Harry feels, but I really think that he's not facing up to the problem. I really hope that he doesn't mean what he's saying here.

Harry: The problem is that I think I am right in the way I view it. I've fought this thing a number of times. Let's just get on with it.

Carl: I'm not sure I understand you, Harry. What things are you objecting to particularly?

Harry: I'm objecting I guess to the fact that I'm on this darn committee. I think that it's a lot of nonsense and I really don't want any part of it.

John: How does that make you feel, Carl?

Carl: Well, I didn't realize that Harry felt so strongly about this, but it seems to me that we need to make the best of what we got and use what we got and go ahead in developing something better. I feel that we should take a look step-by-step at the program we're using and look at some of the alternatives that can be instituted in this environment that we have.

John: I know that it's difficult for you, Harry, to talk about this thing; but I really think that we need you on this committee and I'd like to take whatever time is necessary to kind of get you wrapped into it. I don't think that we're going to get anywhere unless we have you and people like yourself who kind of . . .

Carl: I think that Harry has a lot to offer in the sense that he can erase some of the objections that he may have seen and some of the reasons why he feels so disinterested.

Harry: You know, my mind is pretty well made up. It seems to me that you're introducing what you feel are some facts here, but I don't see any facts. I don't know. Maybe it's the time of day that's the problem, because I have everything going and I'm terribly busy. I have the shop coming apart and here I am monkeying around with this stuff. Who cares? Nobody ever uses it anyway.

John: I think that you should learn how to control yourself a little better, Harry. I think you may have some emotional or personal feelings about this thing. I think you're going to have to settle in and go to work on it.

Harry: Listen, now! I'm not upset really. I don't think you understood what I said. What I'm saying to you is that I'm busy. It's this committee and next month it will be another committee. It's not really you guys or anything else. It's just that it's a pain in the neck. As far as I'm concerned . . .

John: What can I do to help you? Let's put it that way.

Harry: Nothing, really.

John: Would you feel better if we canceled this meeting today and came back later and got into it again?

Carl: Let's give it a try and see what we can come up with. See if there is something we can take a look at and analyze it step-by-step. Are we concerned that the people don't get the right evaluation of the interpretation? Or is the whole evaluation not working well because people resist being evaluated?

John: I'm willing to try it. How do you feel? Do you want to try to go through it again, Harry? Examine it.

Harry: I'm so used to this procedure. I've gone over it and over it. Like I said, you guys talk it through and if I can pitch in here now and then I will do so. But I'm just going to hang back.

John: O.K. let's get started then.

Having read this dialogue (which actually took place in an organization) what do you think is the problem and what do you think needs to be done to improve the way the three men are working together? To put it another way, you are asked to think about the relationships which exist among the three men which contribute to their potential success or failure in redesigning the appraisal system. What is it that needs to be changed to improve the interpersonal relationships in this case? List your ideas here:

1. ____

2. ____

3. ____

4. ____

5. ____

6. ____

The most obvious factors are:

1. Harry's resistance to any kind of change or any program relative to performance appraisal.
2. The pressure on the part of John to get Harry to accept the notion of change.
3. The previous problem which the organization has had in the use of performance appraisal and the obvious fact that these three men are not going to be able to solve the problems without a better understanding of the way they are working together.

The point is that before any serious attempt can be made to improve working relationships, we must first recognize the need for the improvement. Second, we must understand those factors that need to be changed. Third, we must actually implement the change that we think will work.

It is important to remember that we need to be systematic in our examination of the problems we face. We must see what's going on before we can actually correct the problems or bring about the kind of change we'd like to improve the effectiveness of the organization.

We need to understand that there are many levels and categories of factors affecting a problem.

In the preceding case it is common for managers to generalize by simply accusing Harry of being a resister. On the other hand, Harry may be only the top of the iceberg. His attitude and reactions may be a manifestation of much deeper and more basic organizational factors such as the basic leadership of the organization or the rewards and punishment system or structural and role identification problems, to mention only a few. The case was used to emphasize the need for a careful analysis of a change problem as opposed to simply attacking the symptoms. In this chapter we intend to examine some of the factors affecting need for change and to provide some ways to study and understand such factors.

THE FOUR BASIC CATEGORIES

The factors affecting change seem to fall into four basic categories: those involving the total organization, those involving subparts of the organization, those involving work groups, and finally those which are involved in the levels of the hierarchy in an organization. For convenience, we classify these different types of change as follows:*

1. *Total organization:* changes in—
   a) organization climate or culture
   b) managerial strategy or style
   c) relationships to environments
   d) influence or communications patterns
   e) structure
   f) way work is organized
   g) control mechanisms
2. *Subsystems in the organization:* changes in—
   a) norms
   b) structure
   c) power/authority
3. *Work groups:* changes in—
   a) decision-making procedures
   b) norms
   c) communications norms/procedures
   d) roles
   e) authority and power
4. *Levels of hierarchy:* changes in—
   a) influence patterns between levels
   b) responsibility or location of work
   c) authority/power
   d) communications procedures and practices

---

* Source: Jack McMahon, Smithkline, Inc.

e) trust
f) self-image and perceived image
g) control

Although this list does not cover all possible factors, it does represent a classification which may be useful to a manager. The important thing to note is that you may be dealing with different levels at the same time.

Let us go back to the skit at the beginning of this section. What type of change is involved in this situation? You are probably dealing with changes involving the work group, such as the changes in decision-making procedures and changes in the roles of the three men involved. Also, the situation may involve influence patterns between levels of hierarchy. Probably trust is involved as well as authority/power.

A critical question in this case is how the three men can work together to effectively design a performance-appraisal program to which they are all committed and accept. Unless they do find a way to work together, the likelihood is that they will come out with a program which they do not support collectively, and which will be well on its way to failure before they start. You will probably agree that this is an all too common organizational problem.

HEALTHY VS. UNHEALTHY ORGANIZATIONS

There are other ways to take and understand the factors affecting the need for change. For example, we can use comparison as a means to study a well-functioning organization vs. a poorly functioning organization. For example, according to Fordyce and Weil (1971) a "healthy organization" is one that has a strong sense of its own identity and mission, yet has the capacity to adapt readily to change. They go on to point out that the highly adaptive organization is one most likely to search out and use the most effective methods for conducting the business. On the opposite side of the scale, an unhealthy organization is one which typically exhibits behavior which would be characterized as immature or pathological. The significant kinds of behavioral qualities which one sees in an unhealthy organization include dependency, rebelliousness, defensiveness, narrowness of perspective, and general lack of trust.

Some of the characteristics which Fordyce and Weil list to describe an unhealthy as opposed to a healthy organization are included here.

It is suggested that you put a check mark beside the statement which most nearly describes your organization.*

UNHEALTHY

___ 1. Little personal investment in organizational objectives except at top levels.

___ 2. People in the organization see things going wrong and do nothing about it. Nobody volunteers. Mistakes and problems are habitually hidden or shelved. People talk about office troubles at home or in the halls, not with those involved.

___ 3. Extraneous factors complicate problem-solving. Status and boxes on the organization chart are more important than solving the problem. There is an excessive concern with management as a customer, instead of the real customer. People treat each other in a formal and polite manner that masks issues—especially with the boss. Nonconformity is frowned upon.

___ 4. People at the top try to control as many decisions as possible. They become bottlenecks, and make decisions with adequate information and advice. People complain about manager's irrational decisions.

HEALTHY

___ 1. Objectives are widely shared by the members and there is a strong and consistent flow of energy toward those objectives.

___ 2. People feel free to signal their awareness of difficulties because they expect the problems to be dealt with and they are optimistic that they can be solved.

___ 3. Problem-solving is highly pragmatic. In attacking problems, people work informally and are not preoccupied with status, territory. or second guessing "what higher management will think." The boss is frequently challenged. A great deal of nonconforming behavior is tolerated.

___ 4. The points of decision-making are determined by such factors as ability, sense of responsibility, availability of information, work load, timing, and requirements for professional and management development. Organizational level as such is not considered a factor.

---

* Fordyce, J., and R. Weil, *Managing with People* (Reading, Mass.: Addison-Wesley, 1971). Used by permission.

UNHEALTHY	HEALTHY
____ 5. Managers feel alone in trying to get things done. Somehow orders, policies, and procedures don't get carried out as intended.	____ 5. There is a noticeable sense of team play in planning, in performance, and in discipline—in short, a sharing of responsibility.
____ 6. Judgment of people lower down in the organization is not respected outside the narrow limits of their jobs.	____ 6. The judgment of people lower down in the organization is respected.
____ 7. Personal needs and feelings are side issues.	____ 7. The range of problems tackled includes personal needs and human relationship.
____ 8. People compete when they need to collaborate. They are very jealous of their area of responsibility. Seeking or accepting help is felt to be a sign of weakness. Offering help is unthought of. They distrust each other's motives and speak poorly of one another; the manager tolerates this.	____ 8. Collaboration is freely entered into. People readily request the help of others and are willing to give in turn. Ways of helping one another are highly developed. Individuals and groups compete with one another, but they do so fairly and in the direction of a shared goal.
____ 9. When there is a crisis, people withdraw or start blaming one another.	____ 9. When there is a crisis, the people quickly band together in work until the crisis departs.
____ 10. Conflict is mostly covert and managed by office politics and other games, or there are interminable and irreconcilable arguments.	____ 10. Conflicts are considered important to decision-making and personal growth. They are dealt with effectively, in the open. People say what they want and expect others to do the same.
____ 11. Learning is difficult. People don't approach their peers to learn from them, but have to learn by their own mistakes; they reject the experience of others. They get little feedback on performance, and much of that is not helpful.	____ 11. There is a great deal of on-the-job learning based on a willingness to give, seek and use feedback and advice. People see themselves and others as capable of significant personal development and growth.
____ 12. Feedback is avoided.	____ 12. Joint critique of progress is routine.

UNHEALTHY	HEALTHY
___ 13. Relationships are contaminated by maskmanship and image building. People feel alone and lack concern for one another. There is an undercurrent of fear.	___ 13. Relationships are honest. People do care about one another and do not feel alone.
___ 14. People feel locked into their jobs. They feel stale and bored but constrained by the need for security. Their behavior, for example, in staff meetings, is listless and docile. It's not much fun. They get their kicks elsewhere.	___ 14. People are "turned on" and highly involved by choice. They are optimistic. The work place is important and fun (why not?).
___ 15. The manager is a prescribing father to the organization.	___ 15. Leadership is flexible, shifting in style and person to suit the situation.
___ 16. The manager tightly controls small expenditures and demands excessive justification. He allows little freedom for making mistakes.	___ 16. There is a high degree of trust among people and a sense of freedom and mutual responsibility. People generally know what is important to the organization and what isn't.
___ 17. Minimizing the risk has a very high value.	___ 17. Risk is accepted as a condition of growth and change.
___ 18. "One mistake and you're out."	___ 18. "What can we learn from each mistake?"
___ 19. Poor performance is glossed over or handled arbitrarily.	___ 19. Poor performance is confronted and a joint resolution sought.
___ 20. Organization structure, policies, and procedures encumber the organization. People take refuge in policies and procedures, and play games with organization structure.	___ 20. Organization structure, procedures, and policies are fashioned to help people get the job done and to protect the long-term health of the organization, not to give each bureaucrat his due. They are also readily changed.
___ 21 Tradition!	___ 21. There is a sense of order, and yet a high rate of innovation. Old methods are questioned and often give way.

UNHEALTHY	HEALTHY
___ 22. Innovation is not widespread but in the hands of a few.	___ 22. The organization itself adapts swiftly to opportunities or other changes in its marketplace because every pair of eyes is watching and every hand is anticipating the future.
___ 23. People swallow their frustrations: "I can do nothing. It's their responsibility to save the ship."	___ 23. Frustrations are the call to action. "It's my/our responsibility to save the ship."

This listing represents only a few of the characteristics which you may wish to consider and which give you a way to study the need for change or improvement. The list obviously only provides an indicator: it does not solve problems or tell you what to do. It is a way of understanding the factors influencing the need for change. At this point, we suggest you hold your conclusions and thoughts on how to move ahead to make your organization "healthier." Later in the book we will suggest some action steps that can be taken.

OTHER WAYS TO UNDERSTAND THE NEED FOR CHANGE

Depending on your own interests and the approach you prefer to use to assess the need for change, you may find the following of interest. Particularly if you are interested in improving the organization from the viewpoint of more employee participation, the following criteria may be helpful. May we suggest that you evaluate your organization on the following scale:

5 — Condition already exists in organization
4 — Condition exists to large extent
3 — Condition exists to a moderate extent
2 — Condition exists to a small extent
1 — Condition does not exist

Criteria for effective participative management

Each statement describes a work group when it is operating with effective participative management.

1. There will be ample, open, candid communication—formal and informal, both vertical and horizontal. ______

2. There will be "reality-centered" leadership, a use of a management style appropriate to the reality of the situation. ______

3. Goals, targets, objectives will be made explicit for everyone in the organization, and progress in their attainment will be reviewed regularly. ______

4. Areas of responsibility for each individual will be well defined. ______

5. Work will be systematically and well organized, not haphazard and intuitive. Procedures, policies, rules, regulations and other controls will be at a minimum, and where they exist will be the result of collaboration and participation. ______

6. There will be a high degree of participation for everyone in setting goals and standards of performance, decision-making, establishing controls, planning, setting up procedures, defining responsibilities, etc. ______

7. Every effort will be made to integrate what the individual wants with what the organization needs, so both the individual and organization accomplish their goals. ______

8. There will be a continuous effort to foster creativity at all levels. ______

9. There will be a heavy stress on learning and on the growth and development of the individual. There will be a serious effort to help people become everything they are capable of becoming. ______

10. The climate of the organization, though systematic and orderly, will not be rigid and inflexible, but will be characterized by flexibility and adaptability to change. ______

11. Independence, autonomy, and self-control will be stressed, while at the same time individuals will be held accountable for the attainment of organization goals. ______

12. The worth of the individual will be stressed, and team relationships will be characterized by a high degree of trust and interdependence. Individuals will be responsible for their own behavior. ______

13. Reward and recognition systems will be fair and equitable, and will be closely related with actual performance. ______

14. Group cooperation and team building will be stressed and people will have small group loyalties that are integrated with the larger ends and purposes of the total organization. ______

15. There will be freedom to experiment, to make mistakes and to try out new methods—within the overall orderly, systematic effort. ______

16. Management systems will be developed through collaboration and participation, and people using the systems will understand and know how to use them. They will feel they can change them when the systems are not working or can be improved. ______

Total .

If your score is high (close to 80) you already have a participative approach. If it's low (leans toward 20–30) you need to make some changes to initiate participative management practices. Ask yourself which factors are low. How do these factors contribute to the problems the organization is having? What are the relationships of these problems?

If you are looking at your organization in terms of applying Managemen By Objectives (MBO) or a goal-oriented approach to managing, the following scale may be of use to you.

Circle the number for each of the following items that comes closest to describing your organization. If you lean toward the statement on the left, pick a number like 5 or 6, depending on how close to the statement you think your organization is.

1.	Employees seek feedback and knowledge of results. Want evaluation of own performance. Want concrete feedback.	7 6 5 4 3 2 1	Employees avoid feedback and evaluation. Seek approval rather than performance evaluation.
2.	Employees consider money a standard of achievement rather than an incentive to work harder.	7 6 5 4 3 2 1	Employees are directly influenced in job performance by money incentives. Work varies accordingly.
3.	Employees seek personal responsibility for own work if goal achievement is possible.	7 6 5 4 3 2 1	Employees avoid personal responsibility regardless of opportunities for success.

4. Employees perform best on jobs that can be improved. Prefer opportunities for creativity.	7 6 5 4 3 2 1	Employees prefer routine nonimprovable jobs. Obtain no satisfaction from creativity.
5. Employees seek goals with moderate risks.	7 6 5 4 3 2 1	Employees seek goals with either very low or very high risks.
6. Employees obtain achievement satisfaction from solving difficult problems.	7 6 5 4 3 2 1	Employees obtain satisfaction not so much from problem-solving as from finishing a task.
7. Employees have high drive and physical energy directed toward goals.	7 6 5 4 3 2 1	Employees may or may not have high drive. Energies are not goal directed.
8. Employees initiate actions. Perceive suggestions as interference.	7 6 5 4 3 2 1	Employees follow others' directions. Are receptive to suggestions.
9. Employees adjust level of aspiration to realities of success and failure.	7 6 5 4 3 2 1	Employees maintain high or low level of aspiration regardless of success or failure.

There are numerous approaches that can be used to evaluate factors affecting the need for change and thus identification of the conditions that may need to be changed. Two other approaches are presented following this paragraph: the Profile of Organizational Characteristics (Fig. 5.1) and the Organization Climate Questionnaire. In the Profile of Organizational Characteristics, the more you lean toward the right side of the scale the more effective your organization will tend to be (according to research conducted at the Institute for Social Research, University of Michigan, by Dr. Rensis Likert). In the case of the Organization Climate Questionnaire, if you lean toward the higher numbers (8, 9, 10) your organization can be described as an organization more likely to effectively achieve its goals. There is one exception in the list of seven questions that should be scored in the opposite way. That is Item 1 (Conformity). In this case, the most effective organizations are those with relatively low conformity.

Fig. 5.1 Profile of organizational characteristics (From *The Human Organization* by R. Likert. Copyright 1967 by McGraw-Hill Book Company. Used with permission of McGraw-Hill Book Company.)

	Organizational variables					Item
Leadership	How much confidence and trust is shown in subordinates?	Virtually none	Some	Substantial amount	A great deal	1
	How free do they feel to talk to superiors about job?	Not very free	Somewhat free	Quite free	Very free	2
	How often are subordinate's ideas sought and used constructively?	Seldom	Sometimes	Often	Very frequently	3
Motivation	Is predominant use made of 1 fear, 2 threats, 3 punishment, 4 rewards, 5 involvement?	1, 2, 3, occasionally 4	4, some 3	4, some 3 and 5	5, 4, based on group	4
	Where is responsibility felt for achieving organization's goals?	Mostly at top	Top and middle	Fairly general	At all levels	5
	How much cooperative teamwork exists?	Very little	Relatively little	Moderate amount	Great deal	6
Communication	What is the usual direction of information flow?	Downward	Mostly downward	Down and up	Down, up, and sideways	7
	How is downward communication accepted?	With suspicion	Possibly with suspicion	With caution	With a receptive mind	8
	How accurate is upward communication?	Usually inaccurate	Often inaccurate	Often accurate	Almost always accurate	9
	How well do superiors know problems faced by subordinates?	Not very well	Rather well	Quite well	Very well	10

(Cont.)

Fig. 5.1 (*Continued*)

	Organizational variables					Item
Decisions	At what level are decisions made?	Mostly at top	Policy at top, some delegation	Broad policy at top, more delegation	Throughout but well integrated	11
	Are subordinates involved in decisions related to their work?	Almost never	Occasionally consulted	Generally consulted	Fully involved	12
	What does decision-making process contribute to motivation?	Not very much	Relatively little	Some contribution	Substantial contribution	13
Goals	How are organizational goals established?	Orders issued	Orders, some comments invited	After discussion, by orders	By group action (except in crisis)	14
	How much resistance to goals is present?	Strong resistance	Moderate resistance	Some resistance at times	Little or none	15
Control	How concentrated are review and control functions?	Very highly at top	Quite highly at top	Moderate delegation to lower levels	Widely shared	16
	Is there an informal organization resisting the formal one?	Yes	Usually	Sometimes	No—same goals as formal	17
	... tivity and	Policing, punishment	Reward and punishment	Reward, some self-guidance	Self-guidance, ...	

Organization Climate Questionnaire*

Introduction. For each of the seven organization climate dimensions described below place an (A) above the number that indicates your assessment of the organization's current position on that dimension and an (1) above the number that indicates your choice of where the organization should ideally be on this dimension.

1. *Conformity.* The feeling that there are many externally imposed constraints in the organization; the degree to which members feel that there are many rules, procedures, policies, and practices to which they have to conform rather than being able to do their work as they see fit.

Conformity is not characteristic of this organization	1 2 3 4 5 6 7 8 9 10	Conformity is very characteristic of this organization

2. *Responsibility.* Members of the organization are given personal responsibility to achieve their part of the organization's goals; the degree to which members feel that they can make decisions and solve problems without checking with superiors each step of the way.

No responsibility is given in the organization	1 2 3 4 5 6 7 8 9 10	There is a great emphasis on personal responsibility in the organization

3. *Standards.* The emphasis the organization places on quality performance and outstanding production including the degree to which the member feels the organization is setting challenging goals for itself and communicating these goal commitments to members.

Standards are very low or nonexistent in the organization	1 2 3 4 5 6 7 8 9 10	High challenging standards are set in the organization

4. *Rewards.* The degree to which members feel that they are being recognized and rewarded for good work rather than being ignored, criticized, or punished when something goes wrong.

---

* Kolb, D. A., I. M. Rubin, and J. M. McIntyre, *Organizational Psychology*, 2nd Ed. (Englewood Cliffs, N.J.: Prentice-Hall, 1974.) Used by permission.

Members are ignored, punished, or criticized	1 2 3 4 5 6 7 8 9 10	Members are recognized and rewarded positively

5. *Organizational clarity.* The feeling among members that things are well organized and goals are clearly defined rather than being disorderly, confused, or chaotic.

The organization is disorderly, confused, and chaotic	1 2 3 4 5 6 7 8 9 10	The organization is well organized with clearly defined goals

6. *Warmth and support.* The feeling that friendliness is a valued norm in the organization; that members trust one another and offer support to one another. The feeling that good relationships prevail in the work environment.

There is no warmth and support in the organization	1 2 3 4 5 6 7 8 9 10	Warmth and support are very characteristic of the organization

7. *Leadership.* The willingness of organization members to accept leadership and direction from qualified others. As needs for leadership arise members feel free to take leadership roles and are rewarded for successful leadership. Leadership is based on expertise. The organization is not dominated by, or dependent on, one or two individuals.

Leadership is not rewarded; members are dominated or dependent and resist leadership attempts	1 2 3 4 5 6 7 8 9 10	Members accept and reward leadership based on expertise

To recapitulate a basic point made early in this chapter: It is common to see only the top of the iceberg in the manifestation of a problem, it is another thing to understand the factors leading to a viable solution. The behavioral sciences have developed numerous ways to look at organizations, and we have presented a few of them in this chapter. The instruments illustrated in this chapter are like broad indications: They tell you where to look to find the possible causes of problems, but they do not tell you specifically what the problems are or what specific details are involved.

Assuming that you can recognize broad factors affecting the need for change, you need to (1) decide how to systematically obtain the data which tells you what is going on (Chapter 6), and (2) actually collect the data that will help you measure and understand the problem (Chapter 7).

6

WAYS TO COLLECT ORGANIZATIONAL INFORMATION

The collection of data relative to a problem facing an organization is an important part of the Organization Development process. Usually a manager looks at the manifestations of a problem such as turnover, absenteeism, or grumbling on the part of the work force, for example, and from this forms his or her own interpretation of the problem. On the basis of this interpretation he or she then sets out to solve the problem. For example, a manager may observe that a group of employees are repeatedly complaining and grumbling about employees in another department. What they report is that information is coming to them late and as a result they are unable to complete their own work, or they may be complaining about the people who work in the other department (a character assassination type of complaint). After seeing the problem, the manager may interpret this as employees having too much idle time on their hands, which they use to complain and find fault with the way the other department is working. The manager's action to solve the problem might be to load on more work, and thus make less time available for complaining.

While this example may be oversimplified, it is quite clear that the actual problem probably has not been attacked. In fact, there may be relationships between the departments and the people in them which by their very nature are causing the disenchantment with each other. The probability of an error in the solution offered in this case is something in the range of 60 to 70 percent. To put it another way, the likelihood of finding the right answer or having solved the problem in the correct way will be very small.

Organization Development approaches this problem differently. It is quite true that the manifestations are still important. However, they represent only the outward signs of the problem.* The purpose of data collection is to find out what the real problem is. The actual data collection process can take on varying forms depending on the particular situation which faces the manager. Once the data are collected, they can be interpreted by both the manager and the members of the group involved. Not only do the interpretations come from the manager and his or her subordinates, but also the actual design of the solution can evolve from the group itself as opposed to the manager's doing the design work for the solution alone.

---

* Note "The Organizational Iceberg" at the end of this chapter, which illustrates how TRW Systems views organizational problems.

Let's take another example. In one situation that the author is familiar with, there were two factions within a department. One faction seemed to pursue the more traditional viewpoint of "What's wrong with the way we've been doing it?" Another group was attempting to bring about change in the organization which included introducing new procedures and practices. The effect of the interaction of these two points of view was considerable grumbling and sniping at members of each group. Whenever the two groups were brought together in a staff meeting, there was always criticism of the other group; consequently, little decision-making took place.

In an OD approach to this problem, the members of each group were asked to list their perceptions of the other group and the problems they saw with the approach the other group was using. This information was then summarized on flip charts and each group was asked to present its perception to the other group. Once the presentation had been made, the two groups were permitted to raise questions and clarify the way each group looked at the other. To the surprise of the two groups, there was relatively little difference between their perceptions and the points of view each had.

Where there were differences, the groups agreed to look at them in more detail and to work out solutions together. Once this process was started, the groups began to work together in a more harmonious way and over a period of three to four months had developed competencies and skills in solving problems on their own.

The purpose of this section is to examine the ways in which managers can collect detailed information relative to the problems which they see in their organizations.

ACTION RESEARCH

"Action research" is a concept commonly associated with the OD process. It is a fundamental notion about collection and interpretation of data and problem-solving in organizations. The idea was first conceived by Dr. Kurt Lewin. He was interested mainly in social change and felt that the process of action and evaluation, as well as feedback, was critical in determining the direction and intensity of the social change which he was working on. The method he was suggesting started with a basic hypothesis formulation, data collection, and then testing of the hypothesis and learning from the actual discrepancy between the original hypothesis and what actually happened.

To explain this more simply, Lewin suggested that hypothesis building was still a necessary part of basic social research, along with basic data collection. He felt that the data would have a fuller and enriched meaning if interpreted by those who supplied it. The interpretation coming from the members of the group being surveyed may also expose other areas for research. Furthermore, he felt it would help the participants in research to understand the nature of the problem which they faced and would lead them in the direction of solving the problem and developing action steps which they could work on as a total group.

The basic nature of action research is that it is problem-oriented and involves the client's system (the department or unit which is being surveyed). It involves problem-solving and data collecting as a continuous process with feedback and results going back to the group. It also involves development of models, hypotheses, basic approaches to solving the problems, and data gathering in terms of trying to explain what's happening, and it is oriented toward problem-solving. To outline in a different way what we mean by action research, perhaps the following chart will be helpful.

Traditional Research	Hypothesis (What is going on)	→ Data collection	→ Interpretation of results by researcher	→ Conclusion perception by researcher	
Action Research	Hypothesis (What is going on)	→ Data collection	→ Feedback and interpretation by group involved	→ New hypothesis	→ Design of solution by group involved

DATA COLLECTION APPROACHES

There are numerous approaches which can be used in data collection. We would like to discuss some of them in this section, but we must first consider the following criteria for deciding which of the approaches or combination of approaches would be most suitable.

1. *The amount of time available.* Does the manager have a limited or unlimited amount of time to collect data?
2. *The scope of the problem.* Does the problem seem to be very narrow in the sense that it does not involve a large number of people, or does it seem to be very complex?
3. *The amount of data being sought.* If you are seeking a small amount of information as contrasted with a large amount, it makes a difference in the type of approach that you are using.
4. *Administering the approach to data collection.* Is it easy or is it complex?
5. *The nature of the problem.* Is it a specific problem which is easily identified or is it very general and diffused in nature?

Using these criteria we then ask that you evaluate each of the following data-collection approaches to see which one or combination of them best fits your situation.

1. The Interview

The interview method is just what it implies. It is a method of collecting information from a face-to-face encounter with an individual or small group of individuals. The purpose is to get information directly from the people involved on a specific set of questions or topical areas which interest you. Like a questionnaire or other approaches it can be very specific or it can be very general and open-ended. An example of a structured interview approach that was used in one organization involving two basic questions is indicated below.

The interviewer can ask a number of different types of questions such as follows:

1. How are things going?
2. What changes should be made in the organization?
3. How do people feel about management?
4. How do people feel about the company?
5. Who's causing problems around the organization?
6. Who has influence?

7. Who has power?
8. What kinds of changes would you like to make in the organization?
9. What are some of the fatal flaws in the organization that may cause its destruction sometime in the future?

2. The Questionnaire

The survey questionnaire is a quick way of obtaining information from a large group of people. Numerous predesigned questionnaires which have been validated and tested for reliability can be used within organizations. Sources of information for the available predesigned questionnaires include the following: *Instrumentation in Human Relations Training*, by J. William Pfeiffer and Richard Heslin, published in 1973 by University Associates, Box 615, Iowa City, IA, 52240; *Measuring Human Behavior*, by Dale A. Lake, Matthew B. Miles, and Ralph B. Earle, Jr., published in 1973 by Teachers College Press, Columbia University, 1234 Amsterdam Ave., New York, NY, 10027.

The survey questionnaire approach has a number of limitations, including the fact that it is canned and tends to be limited in the scope of information which can be obtained. It also is fraught with the possibility of misinterpretation of the questions being asked. There are numerous advantages to a questionnaire approach: the speed of collecting data, the fact that you can collect data from large numbers of people, the actual ease in assembling the data into measurable terms, and probably the impact of the data on the group itself.

There are many advocates of a "survey feedback" approach, and I think you will be interested in the following article, written by John Aplin and Duane Thompson, which describes the application of surveys in OD.

Successful organizational change*

Once committed to change, an organization must choose a method of implementation. Of the intervention techniques available, survey feedback is perhaps the most effective.

* Aplin, J., and D. Thompson, "Successful Organization Change," *Business Horizons*, August 1974. Copyright 1974 by the Foundation for the School of Business at Indiana University. Reprinted by permission.

Once primarily a technique of behavioral scientists, organizational development is now being analyzed, implemented, and evaluated by managers, administrators, and industrial consultants. In addition, professional management journals are giving increased attention to the entire organizational development process. Unfortunately, the avalanche of OD-related articles contains few that specifically, however, cannot escape the decision of selecting an intervention method.

The purpose of this article is to describe and explore the success of survey feedback as an OD intervention method. The broader concept of organizational development is presented first, and the major intervention techniques are contrasted. The focus is then shifted to an in-depth investigation of the philosophy, methodology, and advantages of survey feedback.

OD Characteristics

Organizational development is distinctly different from preceding organizational improvement strategies. Successful OD is *systems oriented*, focusing not upon micro-units within an organization but upon the aggregate or total system. Admittedly, the bulk of OD efforts is concentrated in components of an organization, but the ultimate goal is coordination of these efforts into systematic change. The systems orientation of OD distinguishes it from other developmental programs, such as management development or supervisory development, which are aimed at specific organizational subunits or strata.

Congruent with the system orientation of OD is a *long-term organizational commitment* to change. Social systems have a propensity to cling to the familiar and to maintain the *status quo*. Inducing change in relatively small groups involves a lengthy process of examination and education, plus the establishment of new behavioral patterns. Consequently, meaningful change in a complex organizational system may take a long period of time and require a great amount of concerted effort. Therefore, OD is not a "shot-in-the-arm" to be endured annually. It is an ongoing endeavor that requires high levels of commitment for extended periods of time.

The professed goal of most OD activities is to improve the *effectiveness* of the organization. We do not plan to become entangled in the controversy inherent in defining organizational effectiveness. Our basic viewpoint is that OD is a process through which an organization moves from point A to point B. The OD practitioner may help to determine point A and assist the organization to achieve point B, but ultimately those points can only be established by the key decision makers in the system itself.

To be successful, OD processes usually revolve around the actions of one or two necessary "change agents." Systems approach, long-term effort, organizational effectiveness, and change agent utilization are all characteristics that demand a significant degree of internal commitment from the organization, particularly the highest levels of the organization. In Larry Greiner's study analyzing successful change programs, it was found that success is often related either directly or indirectly to the degree of top management support.* So closely is top level commitment associated with success that many OD consultants will not intervene in a system without first assuring themselves that a significant commitment to change does in fact exist.

Other characteristics have been elaborated on and are of importance to the serious student of OD. However, given the scope of this article, we have discussed only those most universally accepted. Building upon our brief discussion of the nature of organizational development, OD can be defined as an effort, supported by top management, to increase the effectiveness of the total system (organization) through a series of planned interventions. This definition is consistent with those most commonly encountered and serves to provide the basis for our orientation to organizational development.

Types of OD Interviews

Most organizational consultants and industrial managers are in general agreement regarding the goals and characteristics of organizational development. Furthermore, recent research has uncovered a number of preconditions generally accepted as crucial to the success of an OD program. The most important of these are:

---

* Larry E. Greiner, "Patterns of Organizational Change," *Harvard Business Review* **45** (1967), pp. 119–130.

1. Pressure on the system to change.
2. Significant levels of involvement and commitment of top management.
3. The presence of prestigious change agents.
4. Many levels of the organization actively involved in change.
5. Small units of activity (success experiences) completed and evaluated prior to widespread endeavors.

Despite the apparent consensus in the philosophy of OD and the determinants of success, there is a noticeable lack of agreement regarding the appropriate means to these ends. Various writers have advocated a number of potentially successful strategies, including management by objectives, structural changes, job enrichment or enlargement, technological changes, sensitivity training, survey feedback, and process consultation. To undertake an in-depth examination of all these strategies is not practical; consequently, we will compare only the more widely practiced intervention techniques and their salient characteristics. These may be grouped into three general categories: (1) those relying primarily on some form of laboratory training or growth group as the vehicle for change, (2) those in which the major change role is vested in an external process consultant, and (3) those which use data feedback techniques. The following brief discussions contain the most salient features of each.

Laboratory training, involving some form of growth group, is familiar to people in nearly every organization. The stated intent of laboratory training is to encourage and induce individuals to examine their behavioral styles and personal impact upon others. Through intensive self-analysis and feedback from group members, participants are tempted to alter past practices and adopt new behaviors which, presumably, will lead to increased individual effectiveness and improved organizational performance. In this way laboratory training strives to increase a person's ability to recognize and understand the complexities of interpersonal relationships, thereby making him better equipped for organizational realities.

Process consultation, a method commonly associated with the work of Edgar Schein, involves working with key decision makers in the organization. The process consultant attempts to discover and bring to conscious awareness the interpersonal problems blocking effective group activity. Generally the relationship assumes one of two types: the consultant can work with one individual, in which case the relationship is similar to that of counselor and client, or the consultant can work solely with small groups of individuals as a trainer or coach. A crucial variable in process consultation is the relationship between the consultant and the organization. Presumably the closer the relationship, the more successful the intervention. As with laboratory training, process consultation appears to be predicated on the belief that organizational ineffectiveness results primarily from interpersonal problems.

Survey feedback centers upon data generated by surveys administered within the organization. Consultants employing this technique typically enter the organization at a high level and develop data collection procedures with top management. A survey is subsequently prepared, based on inputs from selected managers. After employees complete the survey, the results are "fed back" to members of the organization. A technique with considerable merit involves a series of meetings beginning at the top of the organization in which all participants discuss the survey results in organizational "family" groups. When used in this manner the data form the foundation for a diagnostic assessment of major organizational problems and provide a stimulus for joint development of a variety of subsequent change strategies. Regardless of the specific process used, the intent of survey feedback techniques is to provide valid information and to encourage organizational members to act on documented problems at the most appropriate level.

Although sometimes considered more applicable to problems related to employee attitudes, morale, and frustrations, or to the improvement of personal and role relationships, survey and feedback techniques have been demonstrated to result in significant organizational improvement. The major advantages of survey feedback for organizational change appear to be the extensive coverage of surveys, reduced resistance to change through employee involvement, an acceptable change agent-organization relationship, and the tendency of employees to perceive the data as relevant and valid for their organization. The remainder of this article specifically examines the advantages of survey feedback and its successful application in a large, multi-plant corporation.

Advantages of Survey Feedback

Experience with a client company serves to illustrate several advantages of the survey as an intervention technique.* This particular consulting relationship began when a company's executives requested assistance in identifying the nature and magnitude of suspected employee dissatisfaction. The consultants agreed that survey techniques would be used and constructed a questionnaire consisting of 75 items. Two conditions were imposed upon the company. First, only items which related to practices that the company was willing and able to change would be included in the survey. Second, there would be feedback of data to all respondents. A total of 1134 production and maintenance employees from five plants of the company completed the survey. Data were analyzed and summary statistics were prepared by the authors. The consultants' role in feedback was limited to sessions with executives at the corporate level. Additional feedback meetings within the company were conducted by corporate managers. Feedback sessions were structured by the consultants to the extent that they pointed out areas of extreme dissatisfaction and emphasized the need for immediate corrective actions.

Within approximately four months of the completion of feedback sessions, the entire company experienced a period of labor unrest, culminating in strikes and/or walkouts at three unionized plants. During this period of unrest, there were acts of personal violence and destruction of property. Although strikes and walkouts occurred at only the three plants that were unionized, there was evidence of unrest at all company plants.

Those plants at which the employees engaged in some form of concerted action were precisely the plants with the poorer attitudes, as indicated by the subscales of the survey. Admittedly, since these were also the unionized plants, the cause and effect relationships among attitude, strike, and unionization were confounded.

This difficulty was partially avoided, however, in a follow-up study conducted upon the company's return to normal operations. For

* Further discussion of this particular case appears in Duane E. Thompson and Richard P. Borglum, "A Case Study of Employee Attitudes and Labor Unrest," *Industrial and Labor Relations Review* 27 (October 1973), pp. 74–83.

this study, eight company executives who had been directly involved in monitoring and in attempting to control activity during the labor unrest ranked the five plants on four criteria:

1. Plant management effort required to maintain discipline at plant.
2. Corporate staff effort required to maintain discipline at the plant.
3. Intensity or amount of physical violence, such as property destruction or assault.
4. Overall degree of intensity of unrest at the plant as evidenced by production slowdowns, threats of various types of employee violence, militancy, or other such activities.

Rank order correlations were computed for each of the seven attitude subscales and these for criteria. Three subscales (pay and fringes, tools and equipment, and pressure on the job) were characterized by statistically significant correlations for at least one criterion. Hence, the validity of information given during initial feedback sessions was statistically confirmed, even if after the fact.

Company executives also expressed the opinion that information which had been generated within their organization was valid and useful in decision-making. This perception undoubtedly entered into two extensions of the original survey. First, the company decided to conduct surveys of hourly employees on a regular basis. An initial "follow-up" was conducted approximately two years following the original survey. Second, survey and survey feedback techniques were adopted for organizational development activities with clerical and managerial personnel. (These groups had not been included in the initial survey.) Even though the project was extended and more surveys were initiated, there appeared to be less, rather than more, company dependency on the consultants. Managers within the company increasingly came to view this OD program as "their" project and became committed to implementing required changes and to viewing this as an ongoing company program of organizational development; this illustrates an appropriate, healthy depth of intervention.

Depth of Intervention—An extremely fine theoretical discussion of intervention depth presented by Roger Harrison provides insight into an advantage of survey feedback.* In his analysis, intervention is seen as growing more and more interpersonal as the depth of intervention increases. Surface levels are typified by low personal risk for individuals, while deeper levels have greatly increased risk and, therefore, less predictable outcomes. Process consultation and particularly laboratory training represent strategies employing a relatively deep level of intervention. In contrast, survey feedback is more surface-oriented in nature.

For intervention to be successful, a consultant or change agent must intervene just deeply enough to affect enduring solutions. A good many potentially fruitful and mutually satisfying consulting relationships are terminated early because the change agent takes the role of overcomer of resistance rather than that of collaborator in the organization's attempts at solving its problem. Without question, deep levels of intervention may be appropriate in some situations. However, since the appropriate depth of intervention is directly dependent upon the norms and values of organization, members may not accept or respond to an intervention technique at a level deeper than that consistent with organizational norms and values. Results have indicated that the surface orientation of survey feedback enhances its acceptability as a viable technique for facilitating change in existing organizations.

As mentioned earlier, process consultation and laboratory training rely upon developing a trusting, helpful, and rather close interpersonal relationship between the change agent and the managers. However, many managers are unable or unwilling to devote lengthy periods of time to developing a close relationship with a consultant. Still others find the relationship unfamiliar and often threatening to their established roles.

Another difficulty can arise where this type of close interpersonal relationship exists, since there is a tendency for the client to become increasingly dependent upon the change agent. If the role of a change agent is to facilitate change within an autonomous organization, should not the goal of such an individual be to strengthen the client system and make the client increasingly less dependent? The relationship developed by the consultant employ-

* Roger Harrison, "Some Criteria for Choosing the Depth of Organizational Intervention Strategy," a separatum from the 4th International Congress on Group Psychotherapy, Vienna, Austria, 1968.

ing survey feedback is more akin to the traditional staff role of providing assistance, support and encouragement, rather than relying heavily upon the quality of the interpersonal relationship. Although additional research is required to understand the nuances of the dependency relationship, it appears that managers are more predisposed to the relationship generated by the consultant employing survey feedback.

Valid Information—Another advantage of surveys is clearly illustrated by our example. To be successful, an OD consultant must generate valid information to assist the organization in its decision-making process. Generating valid information involves providing information that is understandable, specific, relevant to the OD process, and valid in the eyes of the managers. There are significant implications in this definition of information. To be valuable, information must facilitate, not complicate, the decision-making process. It must be constructed in terms that are understandable to the managers and must yield specific information. Of all intervention techniques, survey feedback is most effective in providing this type of valid information. Furthermore, change agent-manager teamwork (such as our example) in the construction of specific instruments not only greatly increases the face validity of the information, but also provides an effective means for building internal organization commitment.

Durable Data—An added advantage is the form of the information generated. Information obtained in a survey is concrete, specific, and above all, in black and white. Unlike information produced in group activities or individual consultations, survey feedback endures and thereby provides a historical record of the organization over time. This is a particularly important advantage in view of the amount of lead time required between changes in certain causal variables such as supervisory style and improvement in end result variables including productivity and quality. By using surveys to monitor intervening variables, such as attitudes and communications, management can obtain earlier information on the direction of change and document the progress of the improvement effort. In the same case example, a side benefit of the survey data was its public nature. During a relatively short period of time, responsibility for the project in the company progressed through three managers. Yet the transition was relatively smooth due to the availability of durable historical data.

Theories of intervention must, of course, rest on a more solid base than that provided by fragmented opinion and analysis of isolated cases. Empirical research is required. Fortunately, significant comparative studies of the intervention techniques have begun to emerge. David Bowers of the Institute for Social Research at the University of Michigan has reported the results of a comprehensive study involving 23 organizations and over 17,000 subjects.*

In this study, survey feedback, interpersonal process consultation, task process consultation, and laboratory training were analyzed and compared to evaluate their abilities to improve organizational functioning. Bowers found that task process consultation was associated with little or no change in the ability of the organization to operate more effectively. Interpersonal process consultation was associated with questionable improvement, although it was apparent some change had occurred. The results associated laboratory training with significant deterioration in the ability of the organization to function.

Supporting our enthusiasm with survey feedback, Bowers associated survey feedback with a significant improvement in organizational functioning. He attributed this success to the extensiveness of coverage of survey feedback, the amount of unfreezing the technique stimulated in the organization, and the organization's tendency to perceive data generated as being relevant to their organization. Our experience and the preceding discussions are completely consistent with Bowers' conclusions.

Throughout this article, our emphasis has been upon the philosophy and theory of survey feedback, an intervention technique we have found extremely effective in producing lasting organizational change. It is our contention that of all the intervention methods available, survey feedback is most appropriate within ongoing organizations. As such it merits thoughtful consideration by practicing managers and OD consultants operating in dynamic organizational settings.

---

* David G. Bowers, *Development Techniques and Organizational Change: An Overview of Results from the Michigan Inter-Company Longitudinal Study,* Technical Report (Washington: Office of Naval Research 1971).

3. Sensing

Sensing in an organization is not a commonly used approach to collecting information. However, it is a method by which managers can inform themselves of issues, concerns, needs, and resources of persons in their organizations. It is similar to an interview; however, it is a group approach to collecting data wherein the manager brings his other group together (perhaps including a third party internal consultant) and poses an open forum to seek out information relative to what's going on in the organization.

In *Managing with People,* Fordyce and Weil give the following example:

> A manager has been hearing from outsiders that recently hired engineers in his organization are dissatisfied. To understand the nature of their complaints he asks the personnel manager to arrange sensing sessions with several groups of engineers and a group of engineering supervisors.

4. Polling

Polling is most useful when a group wants to look at itself. For instance, when a group of people working together feel tense, frustrated, and anxious about working with one another, one of the ways to find out what's going on in that group is to ask its members to give information on how they see things happening in that group. Another example given by Fordyce and Weil is as follows:

> The group has been planning goals for improvement. At this time the discussion is agreeable but lethargic. The Third Party suggests polling the group members on their optimism about whether they can agree upon and later achieve a goal involving significant change. The group consents.

The consultant suggests that—on a scale of from one to 10, with one representing none, five representing moderate, and 10 representing complete—each member assign a number to his degree of optimism about whether they will successfully achieve a goal. The response, let's say, was two and one-half as an average for the total group, which represented a low level of optimism. The next step in the problem-solving approach was to find out what was going on in the group that caused such a low level of optimism.

5. Collages and Drawings

Collages and drawings are simply artistic expressions of problems. For instance, in one organization with which the author was associated, the supervisors were asked to draw a picture of how they saw themselves as supervisors in the organization. Approximately 80% of the pictures drawn were negative in nature; i.e., they portrayed a negative position on the part of supervisors. In one case a supervisor showed himself at the bottom of a long flight of steps with employees at the top rolling stones down the steps on top of him. The interpretation of this information was that the supervisors' basic feelings were negative in nature relative to their jobs. The question they then faced was how to turn that negative feeling into a positive constructive feeling.

6. Observations

In many ways, observations are probably most useful to a third party consultant and less useful to a manager. The reason for this is that a manager's bias perception of his or her own group may be such that he or she does not see all the things that are going on in the group and so is unable to collect sufficient data or correct data to make accurate decisions. Basic observations need to be structured or, to put it another way, people making observations need to train themselves to look for certain kinds of things. For instance, as a third party consultant it's not uncommon for the author to be looking for hidden agendas within a group meeting.

Hidden agendas are those things that people in a group are attempting to accomplish but have failed to tell others about. Hidden agendas oftentimes show up in the ways people phrase questions, interpret the responses of other people, and sort information. In any event, careful observation can lead to conclusions that hidden agendas are, in fact, obstructing the accomplishments of a group.

We have attempted to summarize some of the more commonly used data-collection approaches. Another way to help you think about which of the approaches or combination of approaches you should be using is shown in Fig. 6.1. In that figure we are looking at the use of the collection-data approaches on the basis of two criteria: (1) time or cost, and (2) the amount and validity of the data we are collecting. Generally the value of the data goes up with the investment of time and money. The structured observations, interviewing, and sensing approaches tend to be most productive and the questionnaire, polling, collages, and physical representations tend to be lesser.

Fig. 6.1 Some data-collection approaches

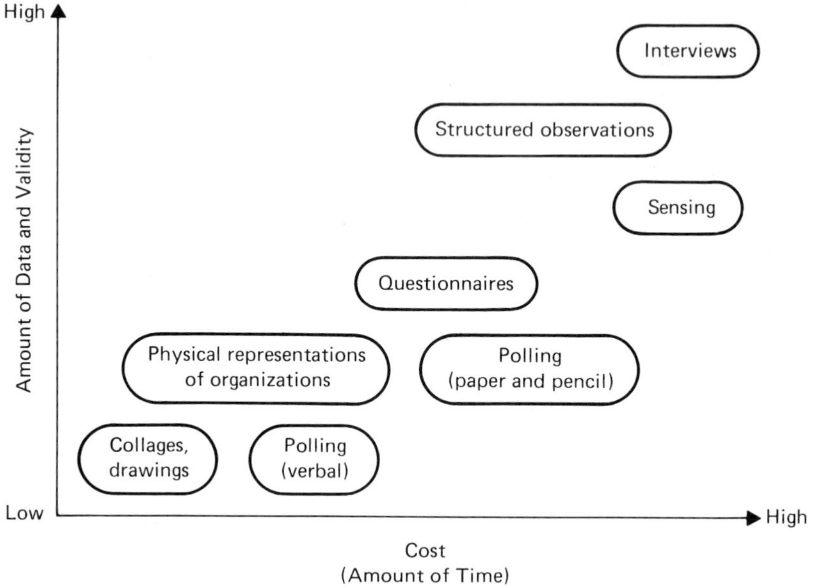

7. Understanding the Data

A word of caution is offered at this point. It is not at all uncommon for managers to think about the information at their fingertips: those things that are readily apparent to them. From these data they generate solutions. The word of caution is that *your initial reactive interpretation could be wrong, and one of the ways to assure that your interpretation is not wrong is to ask those involved to help you make the interpretation.*

The author recalls an example of this from a class situation where he was co-teaching with another person. About halfway through the class one evening the students began to act somewhat indifferent, anxious, and restless. The visiting professor stopped the class at this point and stated that there was something wrong with the group and that he thought that the problem was that nobody understood what the objective of the lecture was. With that comment there was dead silence. Finally, the author intervened and asked him what data he had to verify that conclusion. He pointed out the restlessness and anxiousness of the class. The author then turned to the class and asked, "Is his interpretation correct? Is this what's really happening to you?" The class without exception reported that his interpretation was inaccurate, that really what was happening was that the class was drawing to an end (it was about 9:30 p.m.) and that's why they were fidgeting around in their chairs. They felt that they were completely knowledgeable and aware of the goals of the lecture and that the visiting professor was not the problem at all.

Interpretation by the people in the organization clarifies the meaning of the data. How one person sees things will usually not be how another person sees the same problem. Therefore, the interpretations generated from many people in the organization tend to increase the reliability and validity of the data.

Some basic rules that you might keep in mind as you approach the data-collection problem are as follows:

1. Don't jump to conclusions. Take your time and do a systematic job of sorting out information.
2. Look for hidden causes. Don't take the first thing you see and assume that is the cause. It may be something behind what's visible to you.
3. Check all points of view. Ask not only those immediately around you, but even those you think may have some remote and indirect contribution to make.
4. Look for missing data. Where you feel uneasy and believe that you do not have complete information, start looking for the information. It may not come easy, but it's probably there if you are willing to take the time to dig it up.
5. There's a common tendency on the part of managers to quickly interpret information as gospel. Or rather, they feel whatever information they have is in fact the absolute truth. *This leads them to conclusions which may be misguided and inaccurate.*
6. Remember that data collected in an organization forms nothing more than a snapshot, and that snapshot will not be the same tomorrow as it is today. You must be careful not to design solutions which do not have flexibility built into them. Another thing to remember is that one snapshot will be helpful but 100 will be valuable. In other words, data collection probably ought to be a continuous process—something that is done regularly as opposed to once-in-awhile.

8. Steps in Designing Your Own Survey Questionnaire

Step 1 Decide whether the survey questionnaire meets your need (see Fig. 6.2 for help in deciding which data collection approach to use).

Step 2 Decide what you want to know about your organization.

a) Jot down the points you want included.

b) Ask those involved, such as supervisor, peers, employees, etc., what they think should be included.

Fig. 6.2 Matrix for deciding which data-collection approach to use

Read the criteria definitions and place an X on the line which most nearly represents your situation.

Criteria	Scoring 1	2	3	4	5
Amount of time available to collect data	Very little				A great deal
Scope of the problem	Small/not complex				Large/complex
Amount of data to collect	Small amount				Large amount
Ease in administration, geography, availability	Easy				Difficult
Nature of problem	Specific (involves few people)				General (involves many people)
Summarize your scores (total above) →	5 ↓	10 ↓	15 ↓	20 ↓	25 ↓
This column suggests the appropriate data collection approaches to consider	Collages, drawings, physical, represen-tation	Polling-ques-tionnaire, structured observations		Sensing and interviews	

Step 3 List all of the items to be included in the questionnaire and consolidate similar items.

Step 4 Decide on the best format to use, such as:
a) Yes—no responses.
b) Scoring 1-2-3-4-5.
c) Written (narrative) responses.
d) Multiple choice.

Step 5 Write the questions (design the questionnaire). Be sure to ask for a response to only one thought per question.

Step 6 Pick an overall group and test the questionnaire to find out:
a) Whether it's clear and understood.
b) How much time it takes to complete.
c) Whether some of the questions are now unimportant and should be eliminated.
d) Whether you have left some important points out.

Step 7 Administer the questionnaire. Keep these points in mind:
a) Be sure the responses are handled in a confidential manner to avoid revealing someone's identity.
b) Design a seating where people will not feel pressured to complete the questionnaire in a short time.
c) Be sure not to force people to fill it out.

In the next section we will examine how you plan, initiate, and measure the change once the data are collected.

The organization iceberg* (See Fig. 6.3)

The need is to recognize that all parts of the organization are legitimate subjects for examination and change—not merely the "public" top.

In fact, there are frequently times when a problem or complaint represented *as a structural or policy matter* may really be only symptomatic of difficulties "down below"; or in an organization where the confrontation of personal issues is considered bad form, it may be the only way for an individual to express his dissatisfaction. (E.g., the manager critical of the structure of a reorganization may really be expressing anxiety about what effect it will have on his own future.)

---

* Herman, S. M., TRW Systems, April 1969. Used by permission.

Fig. 6.3 The organizational iceberg

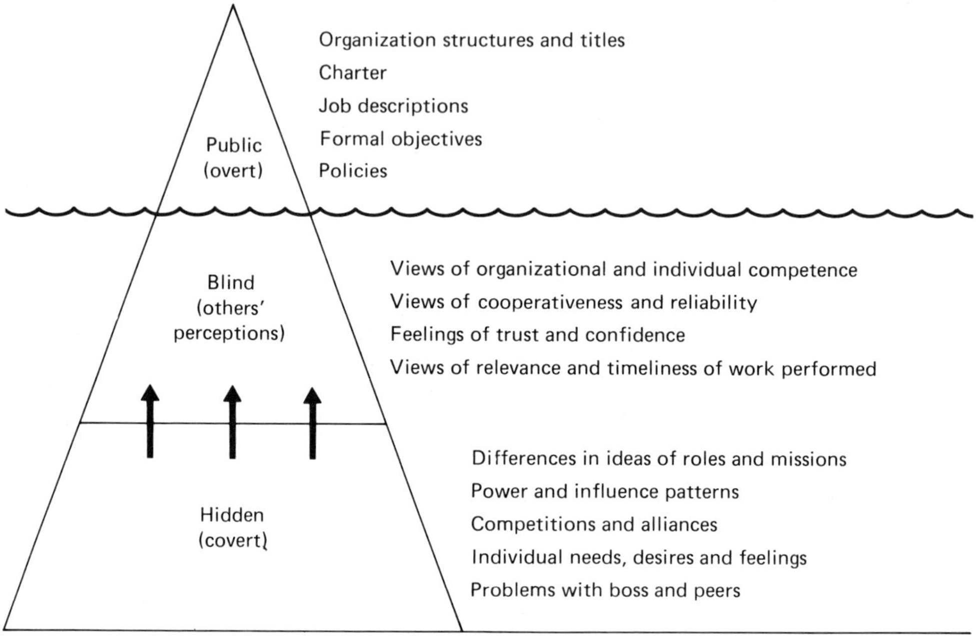

There are prerequisites that must be met before an organization's members can deal adequately with the entire iceberg. These include:

Recognition of need.

Willingness to acknowledge the existence, legitimacy, and importance of feelings as part of operating dynamics.

Sanction and some degree of personal acceptance by top management of "openness" as a desirable quality for relationships within the organization.

Willingness to call upon and use skilled outside resources in dealing with organizational problems.

Some degree of willingness by managers to share diagnosis and planning functions with subordinates.

Recognition of the need for, and work toward mutual trust as an important organization value.

An organization value system that allows members to ask for and receive help from each other without being perceived by others or themselves as inadequate or weak.

Willingness to recognize and deal with conflict openly and constructively, and willingness to examine both competitive and cooperative modes in order to distinguish when each is most functional.

Willingness to risk new patterns of interaction both within the organization and in attempting to change relationships outside the organization. Willingness to experiment with change in behavior styles.

To establish and maintain a truly viable organization change program there must be commitment not only to "away-from-work" team building sessions but also to the change of the "at-work" culture. This requires specific *action planning* and substantive implementation.

In shorthand the process involves:

Data gathering and analysis

Diagnosis

Action planning and trial

Assessment and test

Recycling

7

PLANNING, INITIATING, AND MEASURING ORGANIZATIONAL CHANGE

This chapter will examine the basic factors which a manager needs to consider when developing plans to initiate and measure a desired change.

CHANGE-PLANNING MODELS

There are several basic models that may be considered as you think about the type of change you are initiating. The first model can be represented as shown in Fig. 7.1. Here we are concerned with the conditions which exist in the organization today(1) and measuring the difference between what exists and what the members(2) of the organization would like to see exist. In this situation we want to see what types of improvements can be made. The objective is to bring together as nearly as possible what the organization wants and what its members want(3).

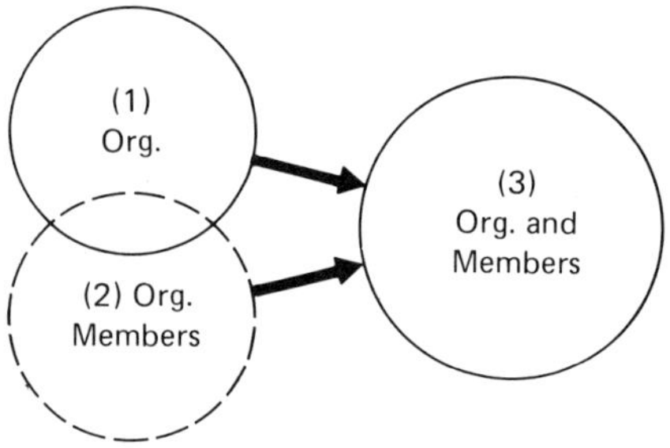

Fig. 7.1 Change model: Improvement

The second model is illustrated in Fig. 7.2. In this instance problems manifest themselves between individual members in the organization (Dept. A, 1 and 2) or between various groups in the organization (Dept. A vs. Dept. B). The purpose in making an OD intervention in this case is not necessarily to bring the organization's effectiveness up to a higher level, but rather to resolve basic problems which exist between people or groups of people.

Fig. 7.2 Change model: Problem-solving

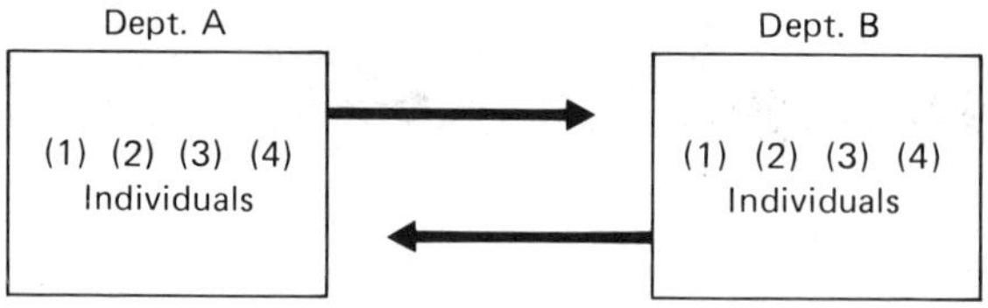

Fig. 7.3 Change model: Outside influences

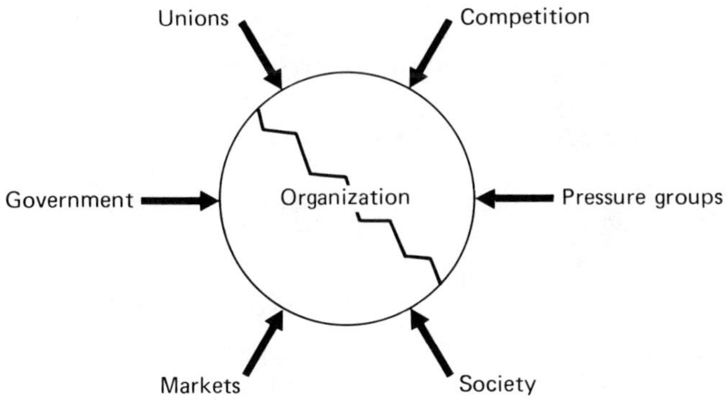

Model three takes a more macro approach (Fig. 7.3) in which the total organizational climate influenced by outside forces may need to be changed. Here it is neither an ineffective effort being made by the organization, nor a specific problem within the organization. Rather it is the influence of changing markets, social conditions, governmental interventions, and the like which are bringing about the change. Such a change as this will involve a far more complex organizational change strategy.

CRITICAL FACTORS TO CONSIDER

There are some basic questions that managers should ask themselves before making interventions. Perhaps the most basic is: "How do I go about finding and determining the factors which will produce data so that I will be able to understand the problem?" Some of the factors which need to be considered are:

1. *Environmental factors.* This may include economic, financial, governmental, political, social, international, and other types of factors.
2. *Organization climate.* This would include the way in which the organization functions, the basic communication process, decision-making, goal-setting processes, motivation, control, reward, structures, etc.
3. *Characteristics of the management.* Here we are concerned primarily with the style of management that is used to operate the company. This includes whether the company is aggressive and

risk-taking and the leaders are self-starters, enthusiastic, committed, take ownership of the decisions that are made, etc.

4. *Characteristics of the job to be accomplished.* In this case you would be looking at the tasks, the types of responsibilities that each person has, the various organizational structure characteristics, etc.

5. *Interunit relationship.* This refers to the specific ways in which the units within the organization function together, how effectively they function, types of conflict they have, etc.

6. *Organizational practices.* In this case you will be looking at the factors which tend to help or hinder effectiveness. Specifically, you would be looking at policies related to the human organization, such as promotion policies, transfer policies, developmental policies, career path policies, and the like.

OBJECTIVES

Once you have a clear understanding of the model or magnitude of the change problem and the factors which are most important, then you need to establish the basic objectives for your effort. Some of the typical objectives for OD programs are:

1. Building trust and openness.
2. Improving problem-solving climates.
3. Making competitiveness relevant and useful to the organization.
4. Moving decisions down the organization as close as possible to the source of knowledge.
5. Designing work to meet both the organization's needs for profits and the needs of people within the organization for personal growth.
6. Increasing self-control and self-direction.
7. Increasing the ownership of organizational objectives by members of the organization.
8. Helping managers manage by using goal-oriented management.

You can no doubt think of additional objectives which apply to your own organization.

ORGANIZATIONAL PROBLEMS

There are some typical problems that managers encounter as they think about the need for organizational change. Such problems include:

1. An ineffective managerial strategy which does not accomplish the objectives which the organization has set out to accomplish.
2. Organizational norms which are inconsistent with the types o. people in the organization today.
3. Inappropriate structures and role definitions (tasks) for employees.
4. Intergroup competition or lack of collaboration.
5. Inappropriate communications system, lack of information being given to employees, etc.
6. Inadequate planning, inability to track where the individual is going or where the organization is going.
7. Problems growing out of mergers with other organizations.
8. Unmotivated members of an organization. In some cases, the entire organization may have an apathetic character to it.
9. Unusual competition from outside the organization in the marketplace.

The above list should help you identify the scope of the OD intervention which you are tackling.

In the preceding section we went into detail on the various data-collection methods which are available. We will not go over this again except to say that the data-collection approach that is used needs to be appropriate to the particular model selected for the OD intervention in light of the various problems you face in your organization.

POSITIVE AND NEGATIVE INTERVENTIONS

Once the decision has been made to move ahead and collect information relative to what's going on in the organization, it is important to recognize that an intervention can in fact cause positive or negative responses and attitudes on the part of members in the organization. We assume that a manager wants to experience a positive result, not a negative one. Factors which need to be considered that contribute to positive or negative responses to OD interventions include the following:

Positive factors

1. Members of the organization take ownership of the OD intervention.
2. They can see how the intervention will improve their job situation.
3. They can see how the intervention will help them in the future.
4. They can see how it will be helpful to the total organization.
5. They can tie improvements growing out of the OD interventions directly to profits and expense reduction.
6. They show a willingness to participate in making the OD intervention a success.

Negative Factors

1. People see the intervention as getting in the way of getting their work done.
2. It is viewed as another thing to do or another "hot" project.
3. It is seen as an intrusion into their own personal lives.
4. It may be perceived as something management wants and not something they want.
5. They see it as a static project which only measures something at this moment but does not measure the true organization.
6. They view it as theoretical, unreal, academic.
7. It is projected as an individual or group's thing as opposed to something they are involved in.

It is important to develop the positive climate that is achieved through developing ownership, showing that the project is a legitimate effort involving the total organization, encouraging the members of the organization to expect something of value from the project, sharing feedback with them about what the program is doing, and finally, seeking their suggestions in developing action steps to solve problems.

MEASURING CHANGE

One of the weaknesses in the OD field is the failure of OD practitioners to measure the effects of an OD intervention. Nonetheless, it is important to try to measure in some way whether or not the intervention is working.

There are three principles to consider at the outset if you wish to measure change.

1. It should not be a one-shot static measurement. On the contrary, it needs to be a series of measurements over an extended period of time. Change does not always take place immediately. There are numerous reports of interventions which were measured at the beginning and at the end of the project that showed no change. In such cases, the change showed up as late as nine months to a year later.
2. Recognize the complex nature of the cause-and-effect relationships. An intervention into the organization may not have a *direct* cause-effect relationship to other factors. For example, improving the team effectiveness of a particular unit in the organization may not improve its profits immediately.
3. Don't try to be too quantitative in your measurements. One of the attempts that many businessmen make in measuring an OD intervention is to try to overquantify it. Many times the best measures are those that are least quantifiable.

Several ways to measure OD interventions include the following:

1. Data such as turnover, absenteeism, profits, expense reduction, accidents, reduced time, and the like are all useful ways to look at the effects of an OD intervention. It is very difficult, however, to specify that a particular intervention, unless it is very carefully designed to influence the particular index you are using, will bring about the change which you are anticipating.
2. Personal feelings and reactions of members of the organization are probably the most useful ways to find out whether the organization is bringing about the desired change. If people are reporting examples of change, then it is quite likely that the effect of the intervention is positive and useful.
3. You may use measurements like those described in the preceding section where we discussed the types of instruments available for

collecting information within the organization. Here you can have a pre- and post-test and perhaps a post post-test at some distant point removed from the actual intervention itself.

PLANNING CHANGE

The following form for planning an OD intervention will help you in thinking about the actual steps and considerations which you need to go through as you develop your intervention. We suggest you use this to develop your strategy.

OD Plan and Strategy

In order to apply some of the OD concepts you have learned, we suggest you develop a change model (intervention) for changing your organization. Your change program should deal with an organizational problem that currently faces you. It should deal with something that *you* would like to see changed and something in which *you* are currently involved. Don't pick a problem you have already solved.

To assist yourself in developing your change program, answer the following questions:

OD plan and strategy

1. What is the problem which is your target for change? (Define in terms of who, what groups, scope, etc.)

   ____

   ____

   ____

   ____

   Describe why you feel the change is necessary and what the situation will be like if the change is made the way you would like it to be made.

   ____

   ____

   ____

2. What is your role in the change effort? What is your function in the organization? Where are you in the power structure? What influence do you feel you have? How and with whom are you involved? Who seems to support or oppose you? Why?

3. What are your goals for change and the needs of the system that you are trying to satisfy (as you see them)? Develop fully a list of specific goals for change. (Include measurable factors so you'll know when you have reached your goal.)

4. Resources: What resources do you need to accomplish the change program?

5. What resources are available to you?

6. What additional information do you need? What approach can you use to collect additional information?

7. Describe the steps you'll follow in your change program.

____

____

____

a) Purpose of program.

____

____

b) Symptoms of organizational readiness.

____

____

____

c) Symptoms of a lack of readiness.

____

____

____

d) Potential pitfalls in implementation of program.

____

____

____

e) Possible value conflicts between individuals, departments, etc.

____

____

____

8. What are the alternative ways for implementing the change?

____

____

____

____

9. How will you measure change?

____

____

10. What's your timetable?

____

____

____

RESISTANCE TO CHANGE

One of your primary concerns should be to meticulously avoid the things which will stimulate *resistance* to your change strategy. Some of the typical shortcomings in introducing an OD effort are as follows:

1. The purpose of the change is *not made clear.*
2. Persons affected by the change are *not involved* in the planning.
3. An appeal for change is based on *personal reasons.*
4. The habit patterns of the work group are ignored.
5. There is poor communication regarding the change.
6. There is fear of failure by individuals and groups.
7. Excessive work pressure doesn't allow time to work on problem.
8. The "cost" is too high and the reward inadequate.
9. Anxiety over job security is high.
10. "Vested interest" of the individual or a subunit of the organization is involved.
11. There is a lack of respect and trust in the initiator of the change.
12. There is a high level of satisfaction with the *status quo.*

The amount of planning and the approach used in initiating and measuring the OD intervention are often directly related to the success of the program. That is, the more planning, the more likely you will succeed. The need for careful thought in planning the initiation and measurement of your OD program cannot be stressed too highly.

8

ORGANIZATION DEVELOPMENT TECHNIQUES

In this chapter we will discuss various techniques and approaches that are used in OD. The approaches described are not the only ones available. Also, depending on the organization and the consultant who is using it, a given approach may be known by more than one name. Our purpose is to give you a general idea of the techniques and approaches which are available. To assist you in implementing changes in your organization, we will conclude this chapter by giving you a specific example of how a strategy can be built making use of OD techniques.

OVERVIEW OF OD TECHNIQUES

Figure 8.1 is designed to illustrate a variety of available techniques. You will note that different approaches are recommended at different levels within the organization. No attempt will be made at this point to go into detail; however, the definitions and explanations which follow should help you to better grasp the techniques which are available.

DESCRIPTION OF OD TECHNIQUES

The following describes seven OD techniques used in TRW. Inc. as described by Dr. Tom Wickes.*

1. Laboratory Training

This ranges in length from two or three days up to two weeks. It is aimed primarily at giving participants a better understanding of what makes them tick and what makes groups function as they do, as well as a greater understanding of interpersonal and intergroup communication. The focus can vary from great emphasis on organizational values and problems to great emphasis on inter- and intra-individual values and problems.

a) *Strangers laboratory.* Participants are usually from different organizations and may include both men and women. Participants commonly have widely varying backgrounds, skills, professions, and trades.

---

* Unpublished paper circulated internally. Used by permission.

Fig. 8.1 Use of OD techniques

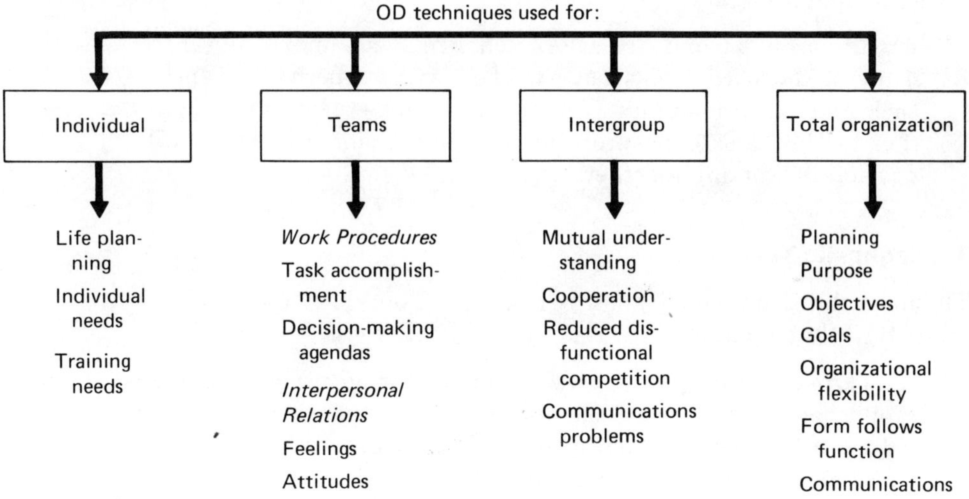

b) *Cousins laboratory.* Participants from the same business, educational, or governmental organization, but usually there are no bosses in the same group with their subordinates and no two people from the same work subgroup.

c) *Family laboratory.* This usually includes the manager and the people reporting directly to him or her. It sometimes includes other vital or key people in the manager's organization.

2. Team Building

Here the focus is on early identification and solution of the work group's problems, particularly the interpersonal and organizational roadblocks which stand in the way of the team's collaborative, cooperative, creative, competent functioning.

a) *Establishing new teams.* The focus is upon the participants and the manager developing a common framework and common goals within which they can work; also on identification of problems which would prevent the members of the team from working with each other—e.g., task forces, proposal teams, etc.

b) *Strengthening existing teams.* This activity looks back over the recent past to determine what the strengths and the problems have been in the way the organization has conducted their business, developing action plans to solve the problems and to capitalize on the unit's strengths.

c) *Re-forming teams.* This is much like 2(a) above, but here many of the participants have worked with or perhaps even for each other in prior times (e.g., because of mergers and acquisitions). The focus is on problems the participants anticipate will develop in working together.

3. Diagnostic Techniques

The main thrust here is diagnostic; i.e., to find out what the problems are with little emphasis on working toward solutions.

a) *Vertical sensing.* This involves interviewing, usually in small groups, an entire vertical slice of an organization to find out the nature of the main problems and the degree to which these problems are felt or make waves at the different levels within the organization. As nearly as possible the interviewers all report to each other in a vertical slice and would be able to discuss the impact of problems as they were understood and felt in the various levels in the organization. This procedure can be carried below the exempt-salaried level through the entire organization to the least-skilled employee.

b) *Horizontal sensing.* This is usually done in small groups on some random sampling basis, but participants come from no more than three or four levels in the organization, as contrasted with 3(a) above. The focus is upon identifying those problems which are most relevant for a general grouping of people—such as middle-level managers, engineers, manufacturing specialists, etc. Though people at several levels are pulsed, the participants in any one meeting are usually from only one or two organizational levels.

c) *Division consulting teams.* A team is usually comprised of a division's general manager, its personnel manager, and an outside consultant. The latter is usually someone skilled in organizational development technology, usually on a university faculty or with a private consulting firm. Sometimes the outside consultant is an expert from within the company, but not in that particular group or division. This team meets on a regular basis, usually monthly, to discuss the current climate or health of the division, to review effectiveness of ongoing personnel programs, to spot new problems, and to plan future actions.

d) *Organizational mirroring.* In this technique, people from a number of functional units within the organization are interviewed to gain a comprehensive picture of how one of those units appears in the eyes of the others. Example: A manufacturing organization wants to know more about how it is viewed by others—what its interface problems are. A sample of people in manufacturing are interviewed to determine how they see themselves and how they assess their relations with other units. Then people from the other organizations with whom manufacturing must work (sales, engineering, personnel, etc.) are interviewed to determine how they see manufacturing. When these results are combined, manufacturing can see from the data how they appear to the other organizations as well as how they see themselves.

4. Intergroup Meetings

This is primarily a problem-solving mechanism. Such meetings are usually held when problems are known to exist and have become somewhat acute. The focus is on putting the cards on the table in such a way that the really difficult hang-ups are spotlighted and solutions, with time lines, are proposed.

a) *Subgroups of an organization.* Example: The sales engineers in a sales unit are technically trained as engineers and have been making promises to the customers about engineering changes in the product without the knowledge of the people in the engineering unit. The focus of the meeting would be on what kind of damage is being done and how this damage can be minimized or avoided entirely.

b) *Line and staff.* Examples of difficulties here are frequent and need not be cited. Because of the nature of their work, line and staff people frequently (though most inadvertently) step on each other's toes. From time to time meetings are in order to help clear the air between them.

c) *Customers.* This is perhaps the most difficult intergroup meeting to design. Usually if the buyer is willing to talk, the customer is not—and vice versa. These meetings should be designed most carefully, and a high level of skill is required. Potentially, however, its payoffs can be among the highest.

5. Third Party Facilitation

This involves the use of a knowledgeable, sensitive, and skilled third person to help in the diagnosis, understanding, and resolution of problems. Usually the helping mode is that of the consultant working intensively with the manager to help him or her work through some particularly difficult problems which he or she has encountered.

a) *Improving managerial effectiveness.* Example: A manager who is unsure of his impact on others, or perhaps of how efficiently he uses time, invites a third person to be with him for half a day or a day. The manager's job is business as usual. The consultant's job is to observe and listen to the content and the *process* of everything the manager does during that time period. Then the consultant and the manager go back over the consultant's notes and the two discuss the manager's style and possible ways in which it could be improved upon.

b) *Debriefing staff meetings.* A manager should regularly use the last 10 or 15 minutes of staff meetings to ask those present what they thought of the staff meeting and how it might be improved. From time to time, the manager might find it helpful to ask a third party to sit in on the staff meeting. Preferably the third party would be someone who knows the group and has a level of acceptance in the group. This person's job is to observe the way in which the staff meeting is conducted and how the members of the staff interact in that meeting. The observer often provides feedback to the group and to the manager at the end of the staff meeting.

c) *Difficult one-to-one discussions.* A third party is invited by two individuals to sit with them as they try to work out some particularly difficult situation. Often this is a manager and one of the men working for him or her. The need frequently arises when one or both are somewhat shy or nonconfronting and find it difficult to discuss the problem. In this case the problem usually stems from their *attitudes* toward each other and *not* the work itself. Sometimes it is because the manager is an overpowering person, and the subordinate needs some emotional support in talking about the issue with him or her. No matter the reason for the third party, it should be clearly understood that the third party is *not* a judge and does *not* have a final say in any element of the confrontation. He or she is there to help each of them say what must be said, to pick up hidden themes which may emerge, and to help them invent solutions.

6. Consulting Pairs

Many times the manager can benefit from a close and continuing relationship with someone outside of his or her own organization (an external consultant). This should be someone the manager trusts, who has a good understanding of managerial skills, who is willing to learn about the manager's organization and its problems, who can help the manager spot problems early, and who can help develop solutions for these problems. One advantage of this kind of pairing rests in the fact that the consultant, not being in the organization all the time, can often see some of the trends and roadblocks in the organization more objectively than the manager. Often a member of the personnel department can function as a consultant to a manager.

7. Consultant Network

In an effective organizational development effort, those who have participated in elements of the program may come to see themselves as consultants to each other. In fact, an OD effort cannot be truly successful unless a great majority of the participants are willing to provide help to each other whenever asked to do so. It becomes a group norm. Once such a norm is established, with little extra organizational effort an internal "consultant" network can be formed. From this network (which is also an OD skills bank) a manager or supervisor can draw the kind of help he or she needs in solving the particularly tough or knotty problems that occasionally come up.

It is almost a certainty that you will find situations in your own organization for which none of these procedures seems appropriate. Your best bet in that case, or indeed in any case, is to get together with your own "external consultant" or OD resource and design a program or strategy which will be as appropriate as possible for your own situation.

Another company, Saga Foods, describes the OD techniques which they use as follows: *

---

* Used by permission of Saga Corporation, Menlo Park, Calif.

1. *Life planning.* This is a program which attempts to establish future directions for Saga people with checklists—based on their current behavior, attitudes, and reactions—to help them determine whether their expressed desires and wishes are going to be fulfilled.

2. *Job enrichment.* This involves searching through the motivating factors in each employee's job and examining the degree of satisfaction he or she finds in each aspect of that job. It then pushes for changes so that the employee can feel better about the job duties and everyday tasks he or she must deal with.

3. *Feedback sessions (sometimes called "Organizational Mirror").* These bring a horizontal grouping of managers together to give data by listening, checking, and testing to see whether the policies, methods, and goals (primarily organizational) are in tune with the needs of those who are running the business, as well as relevant to customers and the times in which we are living.

4. *Intergroup meetings.* These enable two groups to explore issues, problems, concerns, and opportunities in order to see whether or not their perceptions of these are similar, and whether the group members can live and work together accepting any differences that may exist.

5. *Individual consultation.* This provides a "dumping ground" for feelings, and serves as a mirror for an individual to be heard so that he or she can work through his or her "own thing."

6. *Group observation.* Another OD activity is to watch the process by which a group performs its task function, and to cause the group to stop and discuss "What is actually going on here among us, the members?"

7. *Peer coaching and counseling.* This is a helping process in which a peer serves as a listener and mirror for a colleague to discuss personal, interpersonal, operations, skill development and/or other problems.

8. *Start-up meetings.* These meetings help put together new management teams for new situations, such as a new school or hospital account. They focus upon the needs, concerns, expectations, relationships, duties, ground rules, and problems individual team members must face in a new situation.

9. *Group development for training.* We have had some experience in using OD as a means of creating a better learning experience for a group. This was tried with great success at some of our orientation centers and will become a regular part of those programs.
10. *Customer-interface meetings.* We have done some work with Saga's Business and Industry Division in helping them set up performance-planning and goal-setting meetings with customers.
11. *Confrontation meetings.* One of the healthy ways to solve tough interpersonal problems is to have a meeting between the two people concerned so they can confront each other with the issues that bother them. We encourage this and provide a consultant at the meeting to help with the process.
12. *Boss/secretary meetings.* These meetings serve about the same purpose as do team-building meetings.
13. *Husband/wife teams.* We have conducted a few husband and wife team-building meetings with very good results. This can be an effective OD technique.
14. *Unit staff program.* This program is designed to bring OD to production people; i.e., cooks, bakers, salad ladies, and pot washers. It also helps them to become more aware of their behavioral impact upon the needs and feelings of our customers. Also included is what they, as employees, have the right to expect of the company.

Other types of activities and approaches are used by organizational development practitioners. A few of these are listed below:

1. *Employ professional assistance.* Consultants can be useful in organization diagnosis, development of training and education programs, planning of change strategy, and development of more effective interpersonal and intergroup working relationships.
2. *Be consistent in compensation.* In its broadest sense, compensation is a fundamental aspect of change. To be really effective, compensation systems should be analyzed periodically in terms of policy, philosophy, and application. Some compensation areas regularly need change.
3. *Set goals.* Goal setting, or management by objectives, is a management tool which has received mixed reactions from industry

for years. However, using this tool for integrated planning, channeling of energies, and evaluation of performance based on results is both viable and useful.

4. *Develop data.* Gather data in terms of general problems, interdepartmental problems, and specific areas of concern for work groups to diagnose and directly interchange.

5. *Train for change.* Managers need to train and educate themselves for change and change techniques in the same way they need to know budgets, the dynamics of forecasts, standard hours, and cost control.

6. *Utilize manpower.* To support the need for some effective internal job mobility, top management must spend a larger portion of its time on manpower planning and utilization.

7. *Create interdisciplinary task teams.* Many organizations do not know how to pull together or apply the creative problem-solving ability they have within their own systems. Properly prepared interdisciplinary task teams can supply the integration of thinking and creativity necessary for quantum leaps on organization effectiveness.

8. *Improve teamwork.* In permanent or temporary work teams, the focus is on the identification and solution of work-group problems. When solving real problems, natural work teams become more effective and cohesive and learn more about working well together by diagnosing their own mode of operation.

9. *Facilitate job movement.* Increased job mobility is a prime means for keeping personnel challenged. Job posting and similar activities are not sufficient. Policies and mechanisms need to be established which facilitate career movement.

10. *Use a third-party critic.* Use of a knowledgeable and skilled third person for diagnosis and problem resolution can be a highly advantageous way to bring about constructive change.

11. *Encourage self-development.* Individual contributors need to be more initiating and aggressive in developing their own development programs.

12. *Use role playing.* In role playing we act out a short scene. The scene may deal with the past or present, or with an event that is

still to come. Members of the group substitute for one or more of the principals. In a replay, the principals may play themselves.

13. *Get acquainted.* Everyone pairs off with a person he or she does not know very well and asks a personal question or two of the other. A time limit is set.

14. *Use nonverbal encounters.* The team-building meeting makes no progress because two of the key people can't agree on their respective roles and relationships. Each defends his or her own "territory" and people. The argument is apparently rational, but in a subtle way each seems to be trying to put the other down. Noting the unyielding stare exchanged between them, the third party proposes that they Indian wrestle. Once they start, they put everything into it. It seems to make little difference who wins. Both are winded and relaxed. The ensuing discussion is more free, exploratory, and positive.

USING OD TECHNIQUES TO REDUCE CONFLICT

In Chapter 7 we referred to a model or a strategy for solving problems and making changes within the organizational context. We would now like to discuss a specific approach to problem-solving designed to reduce conflict by means of a specific OD technology. The best way to illustrate the approach we'll use is shown in Fig. 8.2.

Fig. 8.2 Steps in resolving a conflict problem

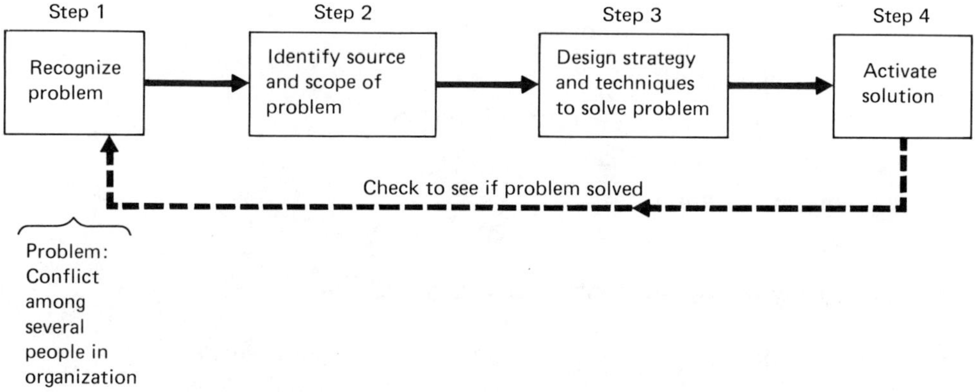

This flow diagram should be self-explanatory. It is useful now to examine how the actual conflict problem is resolved following the steps already given. For purposes of our example we would like to use a basic conflict situation which has developed between several people within a typical organization.

Recognizing the problem. Conflict between people is the basic problem in our situational organization. In this case, conflict is manifested by the following types of behavior:

1. Denial
   a) Straightforward—"What problem?"
   b) By diversion—"Here's the real problem."
2. Withdrawal
   a) By isolation of parties.
   b) Coexistence (distance, denial, indifference).
3. Projection
   a) Relocation—"Don't own my part in it."
   b) Blaming—"Beyond my control"; "They ought to . . ."
4. Polarization
   a) Differencing with high resistance.
   b) Distancing—reduces threat, avoids issues.
   c) Dirty polarization—desire to keep fighting.
5. Coercion—use of power for compliance.
   a) Insist on similarities.
   b) Virtue in submission to authority.
6. Win-lose elimination
   a) Third party decides—arbitrator, referee.
   b) Surrender—better than elimination.
   c) Total elimination.

IDENTIFYING THE SOURCE OF THE PROBLEM

The source of the problem in this situation revolves around the interdependency of people in the organization; that is, people depending upon one another to accomplish their tasks and the feeling on the part of individuals in the organization that one person is not performing at a level acceptable or complementary to the others. Furthermore, individuals go out of their way to interfere with the accomplishment of the work of others.

DESIGNING A STRATEGY TO SOLVE THE PROBLEM

In this case conflict and differences may be resolved by using the following OD strategy. Individuals involved come together to:

1. Define the relationship
   a) Work toward agreement of standards and relationships to protect integrity of both parties.
   b) Both have vested interest in outcome.
   c) Both convinced final positions will respect each other's convictions.
2. Work to remove blocks in relationship
   a) Express your feelings "like it is."
   b) Remove communication barriers (anxieties, defenses, values).
   c) Identify and neutralize defenses.
3. Work to define interdependence
   a) Goals.
   b) Needs.
   c) Resources.
   d) Relationships.

   Checkpoint: Collaboration should become evident. If it is not: (1) Have we done our homework? (2) Have we got the real problem identified? (3) Are other conflicts interlocked?
4. Work to identify problems and resources
   a) About the task.
   b) About maintaining the organization.
   c) About the persons.
5. Begin problem-solving process

Follow-Up

No strategy absolutely guarantees that it will solve the exact problem. There is need for rechecking the original problem to see if, in fact, the OD strategy which was designed has solved the problem. If it has not, then a revised strategy should be initiated.

In this section we have sketched out some of the basic techniques and approaches used in the field of Organizational Development. Sources of information relative to other approaches are available as indicated in the bibliography of this manual (Appendix III).

Before you move on to the next chapter you may wish to inventory the OD techniques you feel will be helpful to you in the OD intervention strategy you designed in Chapter 7. The following checklist will assist you in this.

Checklist of OD Approaches and Techniques

	Application			
Approaches, Techniques	Individual	Team	Intergroup	Total Organization
Strangers laboratory	____	____	____	____
Cousins laboratory	____	____	____	____
Family laboratory	____	____	____	____
Team building				
New teams	____	____	____	____
Strengthening existing teams	____	____	____	____
Reforming teams	____	____	____	____
Diagnostic				
Vertical sensing	____	____	____	____
Horizontal sensing	____	____	____	____
Consulting teams	____	____	____	____
Organizational mirroring	____	____	____	____
Intergroup confrontations				
Subgroups	____	____	____	____
Line and staff	____	____	____	____
Customers	____	____	____	____

Approaches, Techniques	Individual	Team	Intergroup	Total Organization
Third-party facilitation				
Improve managerial effectiveness	____	____	____	____
Debriefing staff meetings	____	____	____	____
Difficult one-to-one discussions	____	____	____	____
Consulting pairs	____	____	____	____
Consulting network	____	____	____	____
Life planning	____	____	____	____
Job enrichment	____	____	____	____
Individual consultation	____	____	____	____
Group observation	____	____	____	____
Peer coaching and counseling	____	____	____	____
Start-up meetings	____	____	____	____
Group development for training	____	____	____	____
Boss/secretary meetings	____	____	____	____
Husband/wife teams	____	____	____	____
Unit staff program	____	____	____	____
Use outside professional assistance	____	____	____	____
Consistency in compensation	____	____	____	____
Goal setting (MBO)	____	____	____	____
Developing data	____	____	____	____
Training for change	____	____	____	____
Integration of manpower	____	____	____	____
Interdisciplinary task teams	____	____	____	____
Job movement	____	____	____	____
Self-development	____	____	____	____
Role playing	____	____	____	____
Getting acquainted	____	____	____	____
Nonverbal encounters	____	____	____	____
Other________________________	____	____	____	____
Other________________________	____	____	____	____
Other________________________	____	____	____	____

9

BUILDING AN EFFECTIVE MANAGEMENT TEAM

In recent years it has become increasingly important to managers for people to work together in groups, in task forces, and in situations where a common goal has been identified. The importance of developing effective teams (team building) is primarily the result of three factors:

1. Specialization within organizations. The need to refine the activities of any individual job into specifically narrower channels has the inevitable result that more and more specialists are being found in organizations.
2. Participation. Members of the work force have shown a desire to become more involved in the activities of their work.
3. Synergy. The benefits to organizations when people collaboratively bring their ideas together are obvious, and the resulting synergy leads to more creativity, more workable solutions, and more commitment on the part of the individuals involved.

TEAM BUILDING DEFINED

Team building, as it is referred to in the OD field, is basically the process of developing a group of people who work together so that they can learn how to accomplish their individual goals effectively and efficiently while simultaneously accomplishing the goals of the team or the organization.

R. Stephen Jenks expresses it this way:

> The goal of team building is to create a work team which functions organically rather than mechanistically. Teams can and do function together relatively well mechanistically when they operate according to a series of rules and regulations, hierarchy of authority, etc. However, it is becoming increasingly clear the mechanistically functioning teams are inefficient [unrewarding to those involved in them] and they produce qualitatively and quantitatively less good work than organically functioning teams.*

Payoffs from effective teamwork as opposed to ineffective teamwork can be seen over and over again within organizations. For example,

---

* *Team Building for Organizational Effectiveness,* R. Stephen Jenks, unpublished paper (no date).

all of us have been in meetings or on committees which have led us nowhere and have accomplished nothing. On the other hand, we have seen groups of people come together to solve a problem and develop approaches and solutions which turn out to be not only viable but also creative and original.

Teams are not magically organized by just putting people together. As a matter of fact, teams are effective only when those organizing them have paid careful attention to the attitudes and skills of team members—including such things as:

1. How leadership is exercised in the group.
2. How decision-making is accomplished in the group.
3. How group resources are utilized.
4. How new members are integrated into the group.

Team building is important to organizations and managers in particular. Today, for a number of reasons, we are seeking more creativity in our organizations. As a matter of fact, our very survival may depend upon our being more creative. Furthermore, flexibility, the ability to adapt to the changing environment which surrounds all of our organizations, is essential. A third point is that we must fully use the human resources and talents which are available to us in the organization. It has been estimated that we use approximately 20 to 35% of the talent which is now available. The remaining 65 to 80% lies dormant and untapped. Another point is the importance of speed in solving problems. The difficulty facing many organizations today is their inability to come up with solutions to problems which should have been solved yesterday. A fifth point relates to the need for *good quality* solutions to the basic problems facing organizations. Not every solution is a good one. Finally, the inefficiency and ineffectiveness of poor teams and groups manifests itself throughout the organization in the form of conflict and loss of interest among team members and general boredom among people working together.

Ineffective and effective teams of managers—or, for that matter, anyone in the organization working in groups—can be portrayed as in Fig. 9.1. When one studies an ineffective team we see such things as people working towards different—even counterproductive—goals; we see people fighting with one another; we see people withdrawn; we see people being directed to produce in such a way that their solutions and decisions are less than satisfactory.

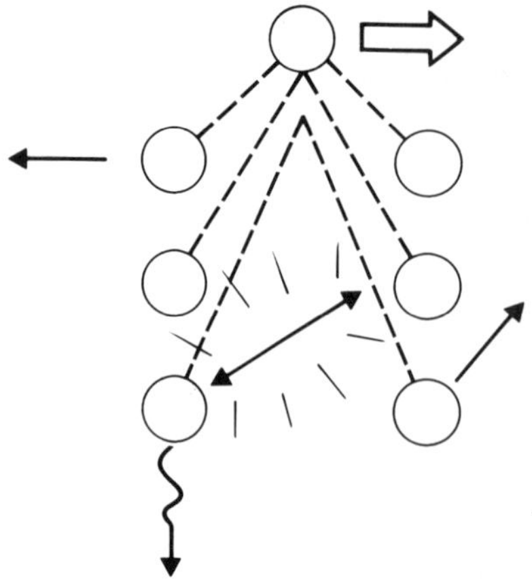

Fig. 9.1 Ineffective teams

Effective teams, on the other hand, can be portrayed as in Fig. 9.2. Such teams work toward common goals and reflect a minimum amount of conflict. Team members show supportive behavior toward one another, indicating that communication networks are open and that people tend to work toward commonly identified goals.

The most basic purpose of a team is to be effective in whatever it undertakes, so those who would build a team with the capabilities of solving problems and achieving goals probably should include some of the following as major objectives:*

1. A better understanding of each team member's role in the work group.

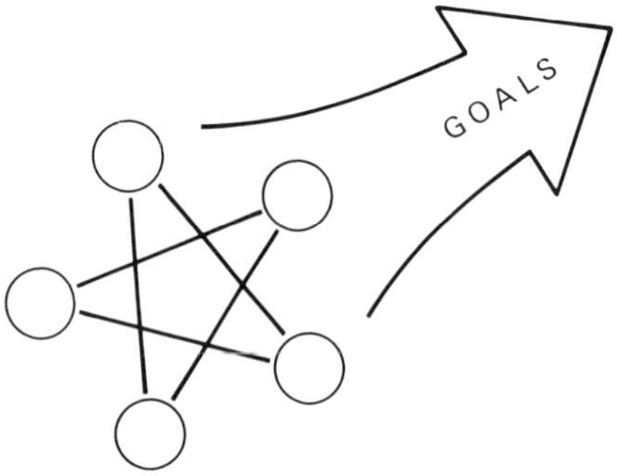

Fig. 9.2 Effective teams

* University Associates Publishers, Inc., 1974, San Diego, Calif.

2. A better understanding of the team's character, its role in the total functioning of the organization.
3. Increased communication among team members about issues that affect efficiency of the group.
4. Greater support among group members.
5. A clearer understanding of group processes: the behavior and dynamics of any group that works closely together.
6. More effective ways of working through problems inherent to the team at both task and interpersonal levels.
7. The ability to use conflict in a positive way rather than a destructive way.
8. Greater collaboration among team members and a reduction of competition that is costly to the individual group and the organization itself.
9. A group's increased ability to work with other work groups in the organization.
10. A sense of interdependence among group members.

The effects of poor teamwork can best be illustrated by using a case example. Recently the author had an opportunity to work closely with a top management group in a health care organization. The expressed reason for wanting assistance was to develop the organization's second line of managers as replacements, since the senior managers were all approaching retirement. After we had collected data from organizational members relative to the best ways to develop managers, it became clear that most second- and third-line managers felt it made no sense to develop managers in the image of the top group since they were viewed as an ineffective management team. The kinds of problems they saw manifest in this ineffectiveness included in-fighting between members of the top management team, undermining one another, unhealthy competition, poor communication, and in some cases open warfare. The second- and third-line managers expressed these problems in a general way by showing no team spirit and a reluctance to work together.

The top management team held a meeting, at which time this information was provided to them. After the shock wore off, the top management group agreed to work on the problems. This agreement came only after people admitted openly that they shared the perceptions of the second- and third-line managers. At this point the top group started to share data on how they felt about their ability to work together. These data included such things as feeling that they had very poor relationships with one another, a feeling of unpleasantness when they came together, actual fighting between one another, failure to share information, a common tendency to one-up one another, and in some cases actual sabotage. In one situation, a member of the top group actually blurted out that she had been angry at one of the other men for the last 10 years for something that that individual had done. It wasn't until this came out into the open that the individual members involved could deal with its reality and begin to understand how each felt. Once this was cleared up, the feeling of anger dissipated and the two began to work together effectively.

It was agreed by the top managerial group that they would learn how to work together in a more problem-solving, collaborative way. They scheduled a series of sessions with the author, at which time they systematically examined the way they worked together and began to develop a more effective team approach to managing their organization. The payoff came when the president called the author into his office and stated that he was extremely happy with what had been done to help his management team learn how to work together. He was very touched by the whole experience, in fact, for the result was something he had been trying, unsuccessfully, to accomplish for 20 years.

There are numerous ways to view an ineffective work team as opposed to an effective one. An example of one way to describe an effective management team is as follows:

WHAT MAKES A GOOD TEAM?

The variables or requirements are stated in terms of ideal conditions as they apply to each member of the team.

1. *Mutual trust.* I can state my views and differences openly without fear of ridicule or retaliation. I can permit others to do the same, too, because I know that no one on the team will "cut the other guy's throat."

2. *Mutual support.* I can get help from others on the team and give help to them without being concerned about prerogatives. I don't have to protect my function against them nor do they need to protect theirs against me.

3. *Communications.* I don't have to be guarded and cautious about my communication. Because of mutual trust and support, I can say what I feel and how I am reacting. When I communicate, I know the rest of the team is listening and will work hard to understand me; I also listen to and try to understand other team members.

4. *Team objectives.* No objective will be assumed by the team until it is clearly understood by all members.

5. *Conflict resolution.* We accept conflicts as necessary and desirable. We don't suppress them or pretend they don't exist; we work through them openly as a team.

6. *Utilization of member resources.* My individual abilities, knowledge, and experience are fully utilized by the team, and I use those of other members. We accept and give advice, counsel, and support to each other while recognizing individual accountability and specialization.

7. *Control methods.* I accept the responsibility for keeping discussions relevant and for the integrity of the team operation; each other member accepts the same responsibility. We don't need a chairman or other devices to control us.

8. *Organizational environment.* We respect individual differences. We don't push each other to conform to central ideas or ways of thinking. We work hard at keeping our "team climate" free, open, and supportive.

There are, of course, other ways to portray an effective management team. They have been described along the following dimensions:

Behavior Influencing Personal and Team Effectiveness

Examine the following ways of functioning and circle the number which you see describes how much of each behavior you show. Then obtain others' perceptions of your behavior.

	Little or none		Some		Much
1. Initiates ideas or action.	1	2	3	4	5
2. Facilitates introduction of activities, facts and information.	1	2	3	4	5
3. Elaborates or builds on ideas of others.	1	2	3	4	5
4. Sets standards and maintains goals, directions.	1	2	3	4	5
5. Clarifies issues.	1	2	3	4	5
6. Summarizes or integrates flow of discussion.	1	2	3	4	5
7. Supports and encourages others.	1	2	3	4	5
8. Reduces tension where appropriate.	1	2	3	4	5
9. Expresses tension where appropriate.	1	2	3	4	5
10. Shows interest, enthusiasm, involvement with group.	1	2	3	4	5
11. Confronts and "mirrors" individuals and group.	1	2	3	4	5
12. Mediates differences, offers compromises, finds new options.	1	2	3	4	5

Analyze your team by rating it from 1 to 7 on each of the dimensions indicated. Then (with the rest of the team) discuss each dimension, paying particular attention to those for which the average rating is below 5 or for which the range of individual ratings is particularly wide. Formulate some ideas as to why these perceptions exist. The "whys" are likely to be quite different for different dimensions.

1. Degree of mutual trust:

   High suspicion ________________ High trust

   1 7

2. Degree of mutual support:

   Each participant for self only ________________ Genuine concern for each other

   1 7

3. Communications:

Guarded, cautious	1 ______ 7	Open, authentic

4. Team objectives:

Not understood by team	1 ______ 7	Clearly understood by team
Team is negative toward objectives	1 ______ 7	Team is committed to objectives

5. Handling conflicts within team:

We deny, avoid, or suppress conflicts	1 ______ 7	We confront conflicts and "work them through"

6. Utilization of member resources:

Our abilities, knowledge, and experience are not utilized by the team	1 ______ 7	Our abilities, knowledge, and experience are fully utilized by the team

7. Control methods:

Control is imposed on us	1 ______ 7	We control ourselves

8. Organizational environment:

Restrictive, pressure toward conformity	1 ______ 7	Free, supportive respect for individual differences

Dr. Chris Argyris (Harvard University) has probably done as much research as anyone to develop a clearer understanding of the conditions which exist when a team is working effectively. He points out that interpersonally competent groups of people (effective teams) have social norms which include a high level of *trust,* a *concern* for members of the group, and the opportunity for persons to express their *individuality,* both in terms of their ideas and their feelings. He further points out that ineffective teams tend to be more *conforming,* antagonistic, and have a higher level of *mistrust.* His definition of an effective team is perhaps oversimplified. Argyris concludes that individual members of a team must be willing to "own up" to their own ideas and feelings, be "open" toward ideas and feelings from other people and be willing to "experiment" and try out new ideas and approaches. He feels that individual team members who are not open, who are unwilling to own up and reject experimentation, are ineffective team members.

Measuring team effectiveness along various dimensions can be accomplished by observation of the team, by asking team members to express their viewpoints about how they work together, and in some cases by questionnaires. In any case, it is essential in the beginning of any team-building activity to determine to what extent the group is working effectively along whatever chosen set of dimensions the team has identified.

There are four basic considerations which are essential as a condition of effective team building in any organization.

1. The need for commitment on the part of *all* members of the group to work together. An example was a group of eight members in which seven were in favor of team building and one (the managing director of the organization) was not. His lack of acceptance and commitment destroyed the total team-building activity.

2. There is a need for development of process-awareness skills of members of the team; that is, understanding that there is a second level of activity affecting the way team members work together. This has been referred to as the interpersonal level or the nontask level.

3. There is a need for people to come together to share ideas and this cannot be done in any other setting than when members of the team are working face to face.

4. There is a need for a third party facilitator whose functions are to collect data, develop ways of feeding back information to the group, and giving the group feedback on how well it is functioning together.

Team building is increasingly needed in organizations for effectiveness and efficiency. This is particularly important as tasks become more complex and more technical, and as people express an increasing desire and need for collaboration and working together to solve mutual problems.

SPECIAL SUPPLEMENT TO CHAPTER 9

Another Way to Understand How Groups, Teams, and Small Organizations Work

I

Several people

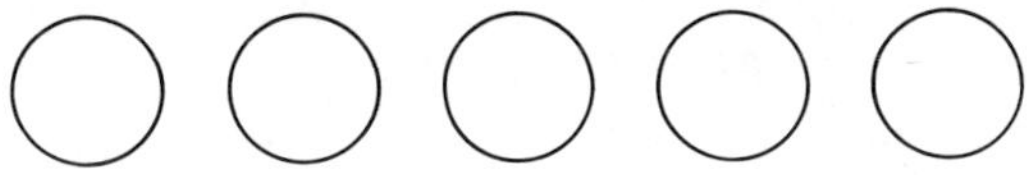

who have internal feelings, needs and reactions,

working together towards a common task or goal.

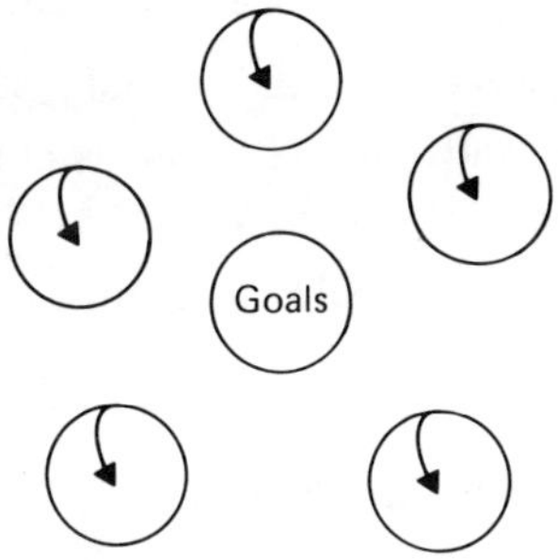

We seldom think of the conflict, the interaction, and distrust individuals within a group may have,

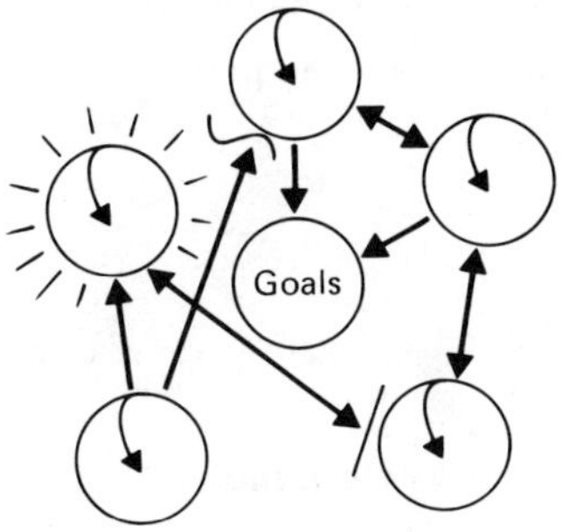

and what result this has on the effectiveness of the group.

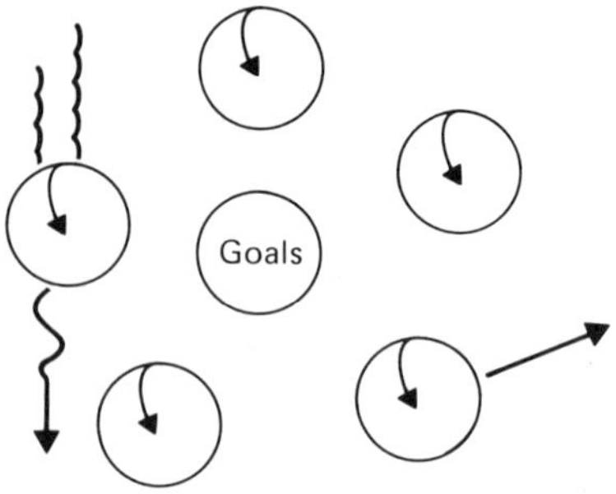

A collection of people in a group, team, or small organization become an ideal work group when they have:

1. A common purpose or objective.
2. Recognized that other people belong to the group.
3. Interdependent jobs, tasks, and relationships.
4. Unwritten and written rules or norms which regulate how members will perform.

We usually say we have a poor team when:

1. Some people don't pull their weight.
2. Morale or the attitudes of members of the team are low.
3. The group doesn't pull together.
4. Some individuals are always fighting with others in the group.

When the group meets to work on a task we usually consider:

1. What should the agenda be?
2. What is most important to discuss?
3. Who should be first on the agenda?
4. How well did each person present his or her report?

This is *content*

II

When we examine why a group isn't as effective as we would like it, we seldom think about:

1. What's going on between individuals?

2. What is the leader doing to inhibit the group?
3. What happens when a group is constantly changing (members, size, task, etc.)?
4. What are the needs, feelings, and reactions of each individual within the group?

This is *process*

If we hold a poor meeting we have probably failed to recognize:

1. Hidden agendas.
2. Emotional reactions.
3. Personal conflicts.
4. Misinterpretation of data.
5. Mishandling of the leadership role.

This is *process*

III

What we usually do to "tighten up" the group for the purpose of improving its effectiveness is:

1. Weed out the troublemakers.
2. Issue more specific and more detailed rules and instructions.
3. Reorganize the team to separate one troublemaker from another.
4. Instruct the group to pull together or else.
5. Remove the leader.

This is *content*

If meetings are not as effective as we would like them to be, for the next meeting we:

1. Draw up a better agenda and stick to it.
2. Threaten to remove from the meeting anyone who shows personal feelings.
3. Be sure that all persons are prepared.
4. Follow the time schedule.
5. Have a talk with the troublemakers and explain what is expected of them.

This is *content*

IV

What do we know about groups, teams, and small organizations?

1. Individuals in the group have personal needs that *must* be satisfied.
2. Effectiveness of a group goes up when members of the group trust each other.
3. Conflict between members of a group is inevitable.
4. How the group is led influences its effectiveness.
5. Member of the group must learn how to work together, which takes time.

Individuals have:

1. Physical needs.
2. Security needs.
3. Social needs.
4. Self esteem needs.
5. Self-realizing needs.

And these needs are:

1. The motivators to action.
2. In effect in some way in all people at all times.
3. Never fully satisfied.

Needs influence the behavior of individuals in groups.

Trust is increased when:

1. Members of the group feel free to express their ideas and thoughts without fear of the consequences.
2. It is the norm to "open up" and give freely of one's views.
3. Members of the group are willing to share knowledge and ideas to help others for the common good of the group.

Conflict can be resolved by:

1. Recognizing that it exists and inhibits the effectiveness of the group.
2. Getting it out in the open and confronting it.
3. Resolving the differences by encouraging the group and its members to deal with the problems.
4. Coming up with an acceptable solution.

Leaders need to:

1. Become more aware of the team building *process* and less aware of the *content*.
2. Identify the factors contributing to an ineffective team effort (distrust, conflict, emotions, etc.)
3. Slow down on traditional solutions (e.g., more rules, reorganization, fire the troublemakers)
4. Facilitate the satisfaction of the needs of members of the group.
5. Develop skills in:
   a) Getting the group to deal with its process problems.
   b) Building trust.
   c) Resolving conflict.
6. Recognize that team building is enhanced when:
   a) People learn to work together (careful—not too many changes).
   b) Goals are clear and mutually understood.

10

A CASE EXAMPLE

In this chapter we cite an actual case to illustrate some of the concepts and ideas which have been presented earlier. We will show you how an OD intervention is constructed and how the OD techniques and practices can be used in an actual change situation. Our example involves a total organization and the changes it made over a period of one and one-half years. The case is written from the viewpoint of an outside consultant.

DESCRIPTION OF AN ORGANIZATION

The organization involved employs approximately 100 persons and is in the computer field. The organizational structure is presented in Fig. 10.1.

The organization is composed of a large number of data-processing professionals and operates on a continuous basis throughout the year. It expanded rapidly from a very small organization to one that does approximately two to three million dollars of business annually. Currently, operations are located in four states with the main operation in a small town in the Midwest.

STEPS IN THE ACTUAL INTERVENTION

Step 1

The first contact with the consultant was made when the president and vice-president of operations requested assistance in conducting a supervisor development program for the purpose of training recently appointed supervisors. Justification for this training was that the new supervisors had come up through the ranks and had not had an opportunity to learn how to manage. Initially they identified the following areas in which the supervisors needed training:

1. Effective listening
2. Writing effective reports
3. Supervisory training
   a) Managing people
   b) Leadership
   c) Training

Fig. 10.1 An organizational structure

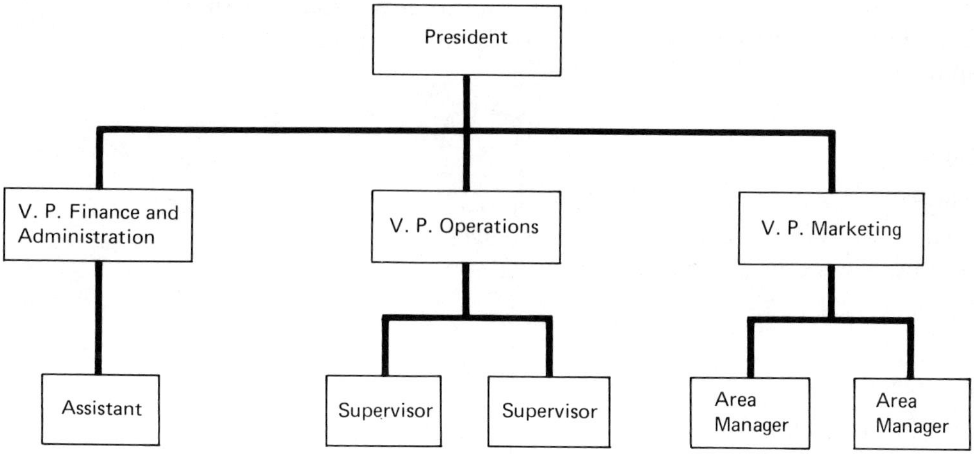

d) Appraisals (performance)
e) Discipline
f) Work standards (quality)
g) Implementing change
h) Review

During the course of subsequent discussions about supervisory training, a number of ideas emerged—including these two:

1. A question was raised about the way in which the organization was moving and how effectively it was reaching the goals which the president had established for it.

2. A number of other issues were raised involving long-range planning and how the organization was going to meet the basic philosophy of serving the customer as well as being human-relations oriented. This led us to Step 2.

Step 2

A second meeting was held with the president alone. The purpose of this meeting was to examine the company's planning and objective-setting process. In the course of this meeting it was discovered that the core problem was not so much the development of the supervisors in the organization as it was the need for a workable goal-setting system. The way the president expressed this was: "Although we have objectives, they never seem to be reached, or there seems to be lack of clarity about what the objectives are." In discussing this further with him, we determined that the objectives were mandated (however suitably).

Step 3

The next step was preparation of a proposal by the consultant. In steps 1 and 2, the entry conditions were being set. How the actual contract for entry was being established.

The proposal included the following:

Approach

Organization change involves a complex arrangement of organization factors. To systematically move an organization requires a thoughtful series of steps involving:

1. Designing an approach to the change.
2. Understanding the factors affecting the change.
3. Systematically moving the organization and people toward the desired goals.

Because we believe that management training in and of itself is often ineffective, we propose a step-by-step approach of which management training is an integral part.

Suggested steps

Phase I Step 1

Meet with top management for the purpose of developing a collaborative team approach to change. This requires that we develop clear growth goals, identify responsibilities and determine how best to function as a team in accomplishing the organization objectives. In various ways the consultant will help you to understand where you need to concentrate your efforts: developing some measurement instrument, observation, feedback, etc.

Step 2

All observations, data, and ideas would be feedback for the top management team.

Phase II Step 1

Goals would be identified and clarified with the second line of management; they would be asked to relate their work to these goals and identify problems they see in reaching these goals. This would involve a series of personal interviews.

Step 2

All data would be collected and jointly compared by both top management and second-line management. A change strategy would be designed jointly which would include those things that both groups feel are needed to help the organization reach goals. It is here that we would likely see the development of a management training program.

Step 3

Selection of feedback and change measurement, desires, and systems.

Phase III Step 1

Implementation of plan.

Step 2

Monitoring progress and adjusting plans as the situation develops and new needs arise.

This proposal was reviewed by the president and he responded by mail as follows:

> We received your proposal and the following are our thoughts and comments:
>
> A. In our eyes, we are going through a management improvement transition that started three years ago. By that, I mean that we need not be "conditioned for change."
>
> B. We are, in fact, well along with both Phase I and Phase II in your proposal. This is currently being done for this next fiscal year with hopes of developing a three-year plan.
>
> C. We think we know what we need in the way of "supervisory training" because of the above accomplishments. With your further assistance and advice, we would like to develop this into a formal program.
>
> With the above comments you probably are wondering why we asked you for a proposal if we feel as stated. We believe that al-

> though we are doing these things now, we need our techniques reviewed and strengthened through feedback and also that we need specific training in the supervisory area.
>
> In light of these comments, I would like you to take another look at our needs. If I can be of further assistance, please let me know.
>
> Sincerely,
>
> President

As you can see it is evident that the president felt that the main problem was still supervisory training. The next step was to restate our proposal in a way that we thought he would better understand so that he could see the necessity of working primarily with the top people first, then moving into a situation involving lower levels in the organization. Another proposal letter was prepared and submitted as follows:

> Thank you for your comments regarding our proposal. I will try to be more specific in line with our telephone conversation the other day.
>
> 1. In Phases I and II we were talking about the way you and the officers of your organization work together and how this influences your ability to accomplish goals. As discussed on the phone, Ed and I feel that there may be some factors in the way your group functions as a team which may, in fact, interfere with the total effectiveness which could otherwise be achieved. The accompanying sketch helps to illustrate our point. Essentially this layout says that people working for your top group will model top management behavior in attempting to reach the goals of the organization. If they see confusion at the top they will act confused. If they see differences between top people they will act authoritarian.
>
> We would like to spend a day with you and your officers to discuss and clarify how you work together so that the message is clear to people below you.
>
> 2. The first meeting with your officer group would specifically strive to:
>
>   a) Clarify and agree on where the organization is going (as far as this is possible to do in one day).

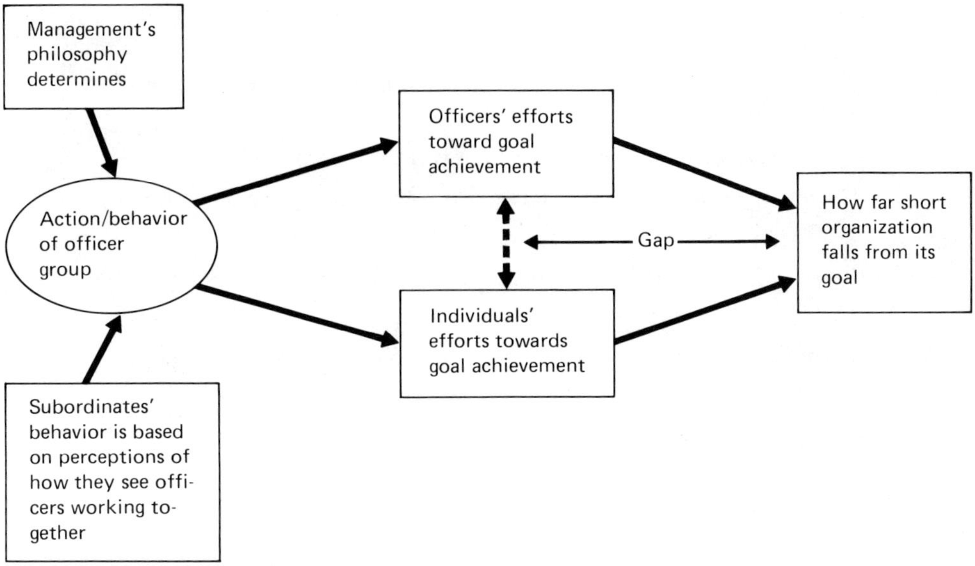

b) Analyze the forces moving you in the direction you want to go and the forces which are holding you back.

c) Help your management team better understand how you now work together and what you can do to improve.

d) Develop a list of things that your top officers feel are needed to prepare and improve the second line of management.

3. In Phase II we would interview those people you have identified as being on the management team (would attend a training program) to seek answers to the following questions:

   a) What do they perceive as goals this year and in the future?

   b) Where do they see themselves in growth?

   c) What are the moving and restraining forces involved in accomplishing the goals?

   d) What do they perceive that they need in order to prepare and improve their own management skills?

   e) What are their perceptions of the top management team?

4. The first part of Phase II would involve matching top management data:

a) Match top management data with the second line of management data to identify discrepancies.
b) Interpret data with you and your officers. Get second line of managers involved if possible.
c) Design action steps including training effort.
d) Set up measures to determine what progress is being made.

5. Phase III is essentially the same as listed in the original proposal.

I hope this has provided you with the information which you need. Please let me know if you need further clarification.

Sincerely,

Glenn H. Varney

The important message in that letter is that employees will model top management behavior. Therefore, anything that we would train them to do in a supervisory development program would probably be a waste of time unless the modeling behavior by top people was consistent. We were trying to encourage the president to take a look at the behavior of the executive group first.

The proposal was accepted and it was agreed that we would start a series of meetings to study how the executive group worked together as a management team.

Step 4

The first meeting was held for the express purpose of collecting data about how the management group worked together. We collected the data by means of two measurement scales (Likert's Life Style Profile and Profile of Organizational Characteristics). Our purpose in using these two instruments was to start the process of sharing information relative to how group members worked together. The data from these scales are summarized in Figs. 10.2 and 10.3.

Figure 10.2 shows the level of formalistic, socioeconomic and personalistic values (see Appendix IV for further information on life style) held by each of the four top officers. For example, person D was low on F, high on S, and very low on P. If a person with these values is matched with a person with a different set of values, then we can expect different viewpoints and ways of dealing with organizational problems.

Fig. 10.2 Life-style profile

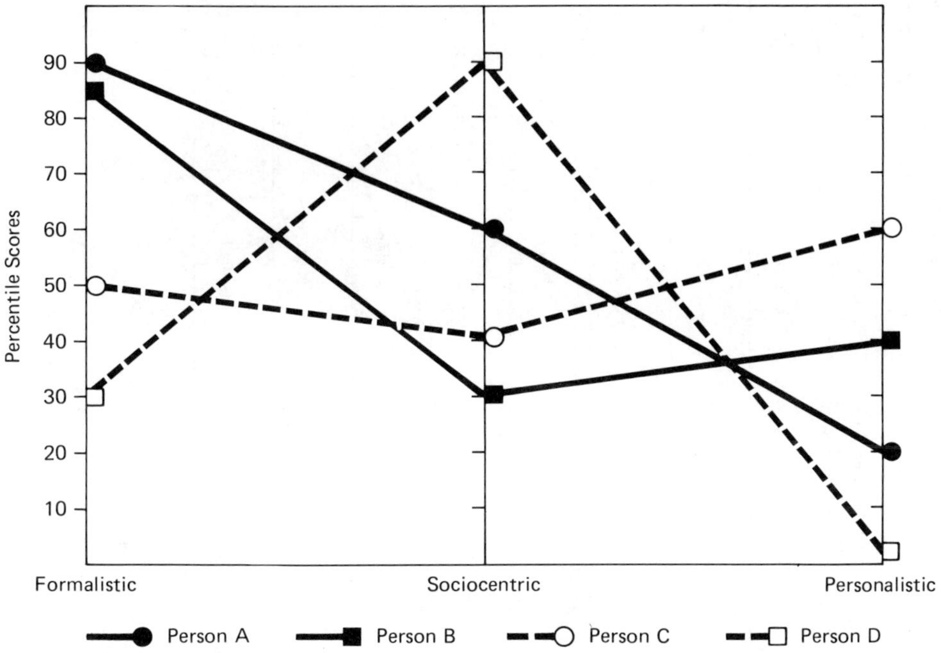

Figure 10.3 shows the range of responses from the same four men on the Likert questionnaire. This time we have singled out the president and compared him with his three vice presidents, which shows the wide range of views of how the organization functions. In this case there are several examples of large differences between the VPs' feelings and the president's feelings (for example, see the first "Control" item) as well as examples of almost complete agreement (see the first "Decisions" item). These differences in life style and perception of how the organization functions help to explain problems that the four men experienced when working together.

A second meeting in a series of five was designed for the purpose of sharing the data, shown in Figs. 10.2 and 10.3. At the conclusion of the second meeting, it was agreed to have further discussions. A second outside consultant was brought in at this point and he met with the officer group during the next series of meetings. The next step was to discuss some of the forces within the organization which made it possible to get things done (moving) or which hindered (restrained) getting things done. A summary list of the moving and restraining forces they discussed is shown in Fig. 10.4.

	Organizational variables					Item
Leadership	How much confidence and trust is shown in subordinates?	Virtually none	Some	Substantial amount	A great deal	1
	How free do they feel to talk to superiors about job?	Not very free	Somewhat free	Quite free	Very free	2
	How often are subordinate's ideas sought and used constructively?	Seldom	Sometimes	Often	Very frequently	3
Motivation	Is predominant use made of 1 fear, 2 threats, 3 punishment, 4 rewards, 5 involvement?	1, 2, 3, occasionally 4	4, some 3	4, some 3 and 5	5, 4, based on group	4
	Where is responsibility felt for achieving organization's goals?	Mostly at top	Top and middle	Fairly general	At all levels	5
	How much cooperative teamwork exists?	Very little	Relatively little	Moderate amount	Great deal	6
Communication	What is the usual direction of information flow?	Downward	Mostly downward	Down and up	Down, up, and sideways	7
	How is downward communication accepted?	With suspicion	Possibly with suspicion	With caution	With a receptive mind	8
	How accurate is upward communication?	Usually inaccurate	Often inaccurate	Often accurate	Almost always accurate	9
	How well do superiors know problems faced by subordinates?	Not very well	Rather well	Quite well	Very well	10

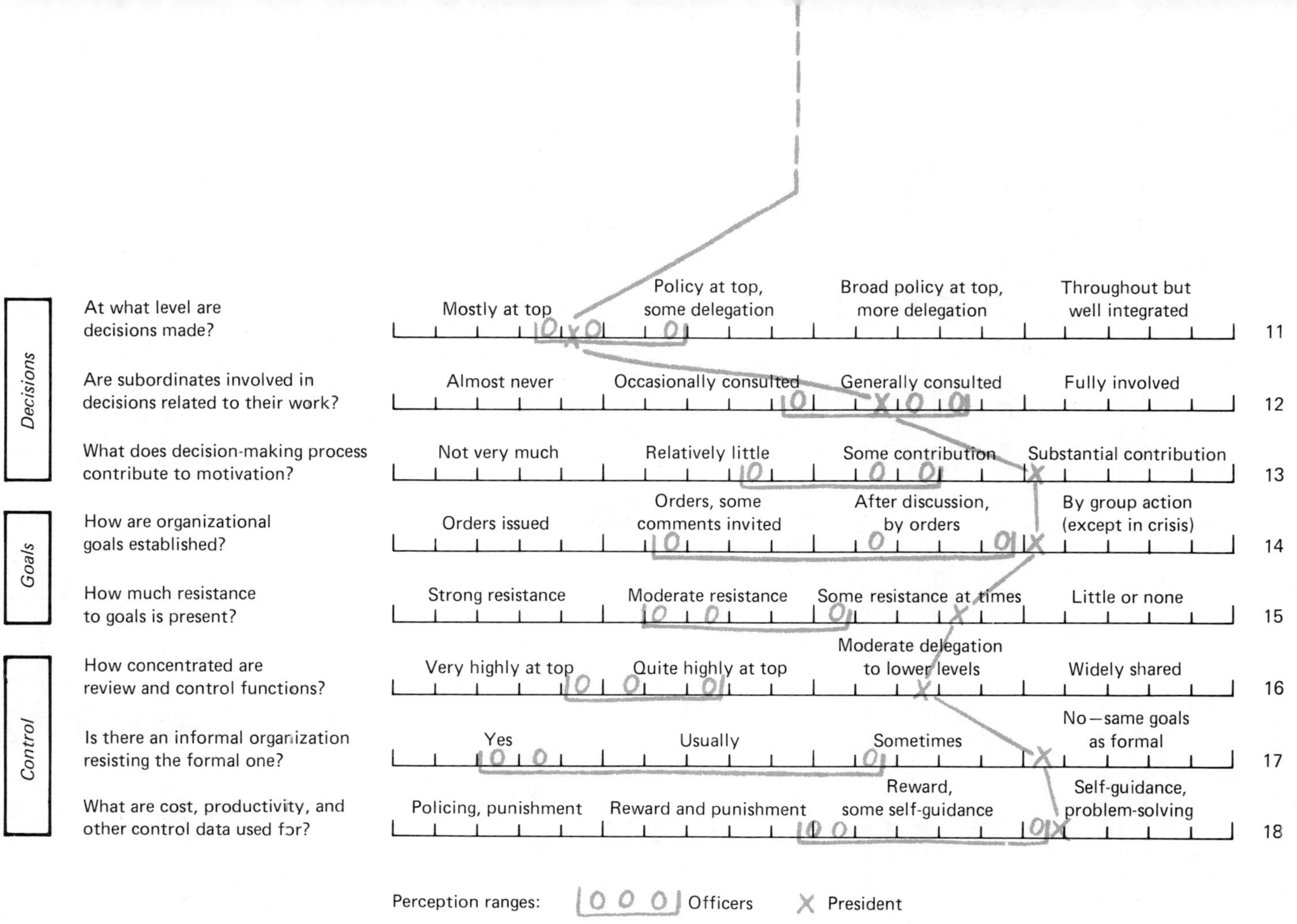
Decisions
Goals
Control
At what level are decisions made?
Mostly at top
Policy at top, some delegation
Broad policy at top, more delegation
Throughout but well integrated
11
Are subordinates involved in decisions related to their work?
Almost never
Occasionally consulted
Generally consulted
Fully involved
12
What does decision-making process contribute to motivation?
Not very much
Relatively little
Some contribution
Substantial contribution
13
How are organizational goals established?
Orders issued
Orders, some comments invited
After discussion, by orders
By group action (except in crisis)
14
How much resistance to goals is present?
Strong resistance
Moderate resistance
Some resistance at times
Little or none
15
How concentrated are review and control functions?
Very highly at top
Quite highly at top
Moderate delegation to lower levels
Widely shared
16
Is there an informal organization resisting the formal one?
Yes
Usually
Sometimes
No—same goals as formal
17
What are cost, productivity, and other control data used for?
Policing, punishment
Reward and punishment
Reward, some self-guidance
Self-guidance, problem-solving
18
Perception ranges:
Officers
President

Fig. 10.4 Forces identified as moving or restraining change in the organization

Moving Forces (Positive)		Restraining Forces (Negative)
Few levels in organization Planning ahead for organization change	Organization Structure and Processes	Time Lack of back-up to train Organized to run an operation and not to manage growth People in jobs they don't want to be in Too lean an organization
Written policies Freedom to run our show Administrative policies/procedures	Company Policies	Location—lack of professional talent Salary differences Company policies not always understood General framework not clear Not enough research and planning before moving
Dedication of current management and people Quality of senior management Competent people Young/bright Trained in company ways Upgrading people (supervisory) People want responsibility People want to be involved in new ideas Bringing in new technical management skills	Other People	Poor attitudes Lack of service attitude Low innovativeness Lack of experience Technical orientation only Company knows only one way to see things Lack of management experience in people Lack of supervisory and basic management skills Lack of openness of some people
I am moving force Desire to be best Willing/dedicated Will accept responsibilities Experienced in management Want to be involved in new ideas Accept responsibility/authority Have personal goals—can be in conjunction with organization Participative management Human relations orientation	Me	Impatience in me Would like more stability Don't always have authority, am bypassed sometimes Not high-risk taker Get into too much detail Not able to coach team to reach goals Giving opinions too early in process Openness is between individuals and me, not group

The next series of meetings was with the executive group and focused on team building. Five half-day sessions were conducted. It was finally agreed that the crux of organizational problems centered around the following points:

1. The president had a subtle power over the officers of the organization as well as over all employees. This power was to move people in the direction that he wanted to move them without their feeling a sense of participation and involvement. Although the president was never fully aware of this power, one of the objectives of the two consultants was to try to get him to alter it and to share it with other members of his executive staff.

2. A number of unresolved issues were discovered between members of the executive staff. The most pronounced of these were the differences between sales and operations. There were very pronounced feelings that the operations people were the "flunkies" or "errand boys" for the sales department and that the operations department was not responsive to sales and marketing needs.

3. There was a relatively low level of sharing of ideas and feelings. This showed up in the way members of the executive group discussed problems. For example, whenever they got to a sticky issue relative to different points of view, each member of the group clammed up. The president would state that, "There must be some ideas, there must be some feelings and thoughts that you have. I'd like to hear you express them." There would be no response.

   However, within 10 or 15 minutes following the meeting, one or two members of the executive staff would be in the president's office giving their ideas or selling their point of view to the president. This led to a feeling of distrust, the feeling that the members of the executive group each had their own axe to grind without concern for the other members.

4. The basic process that they used for working together was highly formal and stilted. It was hard for the members of that group to laugh and "let their hair down." It was not uncommon at all for meetings to have large air spaces between one person talking and another. A very awkward feeling usually prevailed.

At the end of the five sessions—which extended over four to five months—the four members of the executive team had pretty well come to grips with these four problems and had begun to work on ways to solve some of them. At this time the top group made a conscientious decision to move further into the organization—and this led to Step 5.

Step 5

It was agreed that we would move to the next level, bringing in five additional members of management. The objectives of this move were to: (1) link up and integrate the second line of management with the top management group and (2) build a "total team" approach to operating the company, wherein the second group would actively participate in managing the organization.

To achieve these objectives we developed two different and independent strategies. Strategy 1, which we presented at the September 30th meeting, was as follows:

1. Design questions to use in interviews. Summarize top management's perceptions of second-line management.
2. Select questions and validate perceptions.
3. Interview five men, individually or in a group.
4. Share data with top management.
5. Have the group of nine share data and discuss it.
6. Plan alternative steps.

Strategy 2 consisted of a one-day meeting during which all nine people would share perceptions and plan action steps. The course of action for such a day could take the following form:

1. Purpose/plan for the day.
2. Measurements: Use instruments designed to measure selected key managerial variables for each group.
3. Each group summarizes and shares data.
4. Each group interprets and clarifies the data of the other group.
5. The total group selects key areas to be worked on.
6. The total group designs action plans and commits itself to accept responsibility and to follow up on the plans.
7. Future plans.

Strategy 2 was chosen and implemented several weeks later. The actual schedule of activities for that one-day meeting was as follows:

1. Introduction—statement by president

a) Purpose of session
b) Our role—your roles
c) How we will work
d) What we will do
e) Outcome

2. Life style
   a) Purpose: establish collaborative approach today
   b) Questionnaire
   c) Profile (identify by name)
      1) Flipchart
      2) Small group
      3) Report to total group (share)

3. Questionnaire administered

4. Share data (small group position report)
   a) Collecting and summarizing data
   b) Study: Identify and interpret significant points
   c) Discussion. Purpose: to identify specific things that provide examples.
   d) What do you want to say to other group?

From this second strategy came data similar to the data created in the officers' meetings. The method used to generate the data involved an open, confronting, sharing process in which members of the management team openly disclosed information about their feelings and ideas. Some of the information that surfaced was:

1. Major areas of concern to total management group:
   a) Lack of clarity of expectations each has for the other person.
   b) Making commitment without taking time at "front end" to understand specifics.
   c) Need for moving toward improved teamwork and a lower level of frustration.
   d) President has not encouraged close professional (career) and personal relationships.
   e) I have confidence in my people but I do not have confidence in others, subordinates.
   f) People tend to be reactive.

1) All related to lack of involvement and working together (i.e., this session).
2) Also due to lack of managers and general work experience (personal career development).
3) Seeming lack of desire for self-improvement.

g) You end up committed to something without understanding it.

h) What to work on is not clear in some cases, but we think it should be worked out individually by those involved.

i) Recognition of performance, right or wrong, inadequate at best. Everybody wants a pat on the back or kita. Criticism is nonexistent, praise is low.

j) Uneasy about what we don't know. Not much is done to find out what we're uneasy about.

k) Can't trust the corporate file to include everything.

l) You end up embarrassed to explain something after it's happened.

m) Perceptions of management group:

1) Cooperation: the clashes are strong and the harmony is forced. Feel progress is being made.
2) Good competent men. We need to initiate more at tying down loose ends to balance self-starters with finishers.
3) Great with ideas—slow acceptance takes away from impact.
4) Communication is active, open but not always complete.
5) Feeling of frustration with others' unwillingness to listen. Frustration is high but progress is felt.

n) Characteristics of top and second-line managers:

1) Emphasis is on growth, direction, profit. The employee emphasis has moved from 0 to midpoint over last several years.
2) Organization problems get backseated to customer, profit, growth, and the future.
3) Unintentionally we're overlooking objectives and overemphasizing profit.
4) Take-charge attitude needs to be correlated to end results.

At the conclusion of the meeting a number of decisions were reached which served as a set of action steps that the management team were now committed to work on:

Decision 1—

a) *We* need to clarify what we are doing.

b) We need to learn more about *how* we work and communicate together.

Decision 2—Suggested areas to work on:

a) Pay more attention to solving interpersonal problems (IP).

b) Learn how to solve interpersonal problems *face to face.*

1) Go direct.

2) Problem-solve (not criticize).

Decision 3—What has to be done to improve our management skill?

a) More information.

b) More involvement.

c) Closer contact on career and personal development.

Decision 4—Design together an information-sharing system that gives each of us what we need. (Increase confidence in system.)

a) Use corporation file more effectively.

b) Develop other systems if needed.

Decision 5—Share like data generated today on a one-to-one basis.

The general reaction to the one-day meeting was that it was highly successful and that the management team had now progressed to a new level of teamwork which would foster a more effective management effort.

Several weeks later it was clear that the total group was moving ahead with their decisions and that they felt problems were being faced squarely and resolved. Furthermore, they subsequently decided to conduct a total organization climate survey for the purpose of collecting data relative to how people, in general, felt about the organization.

A year later there was still a strong feeling that the initial OD intervention paid off both in the way people feel about their work and in the way they work together. There was clearly a more intense sense of involvement. There was more excitement in the organization and a feeling that things were moving ahead. Indeed, it appeared that this intervention was working well for this particular organization.

11

INSTALLING AN ORGANIZATION DEVELOPMENT PROGRAM

In this final chapter we will summarize several points which we discussed earlier. In particular, we want to talk about the considerations that need to be noted as you start to use an OD approach to organizational change. We would also like to discuss some of the skills that a person needs to develop in order to be able to make changes. We will also set forth a job description for a person responsible for Organization Development.

We will discuss several important questions in the establishment of an internal OD consulting capability. We'll go through a set of steps involved in the installation of an Organization Development approach, list some conditions for successful and unsuccessful OD interventions, and conclude by presenting an OD planning form which can be used to analyze your own OD approach.

FACTORS TO CONSIDER WHEN INSTALLING AN OD PROGRAM

There are a number of factors that need to be considered, some of which have been previously mentioned and summarized here. These are as follows:

1. There should be a strong need for change within your organization. In other words, there needs to be a general consensus from members of the organization that some improvement is necessary and the change is desirable.
2. The top level of management needs to be involved. This does not necessarily mean the president of the organization; however, it does mean top levels in the organization including the person responsible for the unit that may be involved. Commitment of top management is essential, since many of the problems which will be uncovered will require agreement and participation on the part of top management.
3. There's a need for almost total commitment on the part of the organization. By total, we do not mean 100% of the organization, but we do believe that at least a majority of the people in the target system must be solidly behind an OD effort.
4. The organizational development objectives need to be clear. What is it that you are trying to accomplish and what do you hope to have as an end result from the OD program?
5. You need to ask the question, "Are we changing values of people in the organization or are we attempting to change behavior?"

It has long been recognized that attempting to change values of people in an organization is oftentimes a futile effort. Changing behavior, on the other hand, is quite feasible. This means that people would change their relationships—the way in which they work together, the things they do with one another—rather than the things that they believe in.

6. Are the OD effort you are embarking upon and the ideas you have to include in the OD program unique to your organization or are they ideas which have been lifted from some other organization because they seem to work well there?

7. You must decide whether you need outside professional help or whether you can make the necessary change from within the organization. Depending on the magnitude of the problem and the abilities of the people in the organization, it might be advisable to seek professional OD help from outside.

8. Does your program focus on individual behavior or on structural and systems types of activities? Most OD practitioners would agree that the systems and organizational structure have a bearing on a change strategy on which you embark. But generally speaking, OD efforts focus on individual behavior rather than on systems behavior.

9. Is your OD effort a long-term commitment or is it designed to solve an immediate problem in order to get on with the daily work which needs to be accomplished? If it is a short-term commitment, probably you should not consider OD as a strategy for bringing about the change.

10. In no case should you go into an OD effort without attempting to measure the effect or the change which is a result of the OD program. This, of course, will not be as easy for you to do as it is for us to talk about it. On the other hand, it is essential that you recognize the changes which you are after. If you are unable to measure them, then you are likely not experiencing any changes at all.

CHANGE AGENT SKILLS

Jennings Partin (1973) lists seven basic skills and areas of knowledge which a person making change in his organization should have. These are summarized on the next page.

Skill Area 1. "Assessment by the change agent of his personal motivation and his relationships to the 'changee'." We interpret this to mean that before you embark on an OD effort you should be very clear about your role as the change agent in moving the organization from one point to another. This includes such considerations as your own personal development, your personal professional goals, your interest in the organization as a whole, etc.

Skill Area 2. "Helping changes become aware of the need for change and for the diagnostic process." In this case we believe that Partin alludes to the fact that a manager should be concerned about helping people in his or her organization to become aware of the problems which face them and the fact that they can, through their own diagnostic abilities, solve the problems.

Skill Area 3. "Diagnosis by changer and changee in collaboration concerning the situation, behavior, understanding, feeling, or performance to be modified." This would include such things as diagnosis in terms of causes rather than goods or bads, skills in helping changees to examine their own motivation, clarification of relationships or roles between changer and changee, and so forth.

Skill Area 4. "Deciding upon the problems; involving others in this decision; planning and implementing action." In this case we are talking about making a step-by-step plan, planning and providing administrative organization to implement the change, eliciting and eliminating the various alternatives; in other words, using a systematic approach to examining the problem.

Skill Area 5. "Carrying out the plan successfully and productively." Here reference is made to having a clear understanding of what it takes to solve the problem, particularly understanding the effects of the alternate approaches which are being proposed for the change.

Skill Area 6. "Evaluation and assessment of changees' progress, methods of working, and human relations." As we previously mentioned, we are talking about now being sure that you have your sights on the change or goal which you are attempting to accomplish.

Skill Area 7. "Ensuring continuity . . . and transfer." The skills required for this area are accurate perceptions and responsibility for participation on the part of the persons being developed. There must also be a clear understanding of the degree of general support needed for the change, as well as an appreciation by others of the work of those participants who need the support.

SETTING UP AN INTERNAL OD CONSULTING ORGANIZATION

One of the first questions a manager needs to ask himself or herself is: "Should I have an inside (within the organization) competency in OD?" The answer to this may be, "No, I do not need such competency; I can manage it myself." However, organizations will generally find that they do need some inside and perhaps some outside help. One of the common ways for developing inside expertise is to develop an in organization OD team. Some of the arguments for an inside team as opposed to outside assistance include their knowledge of the company, their availability, and the commitment they have to solving the problem.

The nature of an inside consulting organization should not be a typical staff relationship but a consulting relationship. The difference is that the departmental members or units within the organization hire the internal OD specialist as a consultant, instead of themselves imposing staff competency and skills on their subordinates. Consultants are freer to say what they have to say without fear of reprisal from the organization. Their ability to work effectively in the organization—or to put it another way, the power they acquire by being able to solve problems and help the organization—is vested primarily in their ability to help. Such a group should not be organizationally bound. They should not be restricted to looking only at the inside of the organization as a way to solve the problems, but should be allowed to work outside with other organizations. These could include academic institutions and other consultants, for example, as well as other businesses or industries. The benefits of this are clear: Contacts and opportunities to work with people outside the organization all help to broaden the perspective of the inside OD group.

An internal consulting group probably should be established high in the organization, preferably at the presidential level. Generally speaking, OD consultants are most effective if not assigned to the personnel department, but this is not an inflexible rule. As a matter of fact, a large percentage of the OD internal consultants are working in personnel activities. Whether they should be assigned to the personnel department or to a staff officer largely depends on how well accepted the personnel department is. If it is a weak department not considered effective and useful in the organization, then perhaps the OD effort should be assigned elsewhere, to someone such as the president or vice-president.

Jennings Partin provides a typical job description for an OD internal consultant:*

1. *Charter*

   To help develop a full functioning organization whose goals and objectives are achieved through optimal use of its human and material resources. Organization planning and systems development are primarily the responsibility of operating management. The role of the organization and systems group is to provide technical assistance to management for achieving its goals and objectives. This group serves as an internal consultant to line management on a variety of issues regarding (1) organization structuring, (2) management system design, (3) performance evaluation, and (4) problems that often involve interfacing groups.

2. *Goals*

   1. To develop a fully functioning organization that optimizes its human and material resources in accomplishing its specific goals and objectives.
   2. To develop a work climate built on openness, trust, and respect for individual members.
   3. To develop an active organization that anticipates problems before they occur and plans for them as soon as it is realistically possible to do so.
   4. To affix appropriate authorities and responsibilities for organization members and facilitate the development of a work climate that encourages individual initiative and personal fulfillment.
   5. To create, develop and maintain effective management systems that are designed to facilitate optimal organization performance.

3. *Responsibilities and Authorities*

   1. Assist management in diagnosing organization or system problems and implementing plans to overcome them.

---

* Partin, J. Jennings, *Current Perspectives in Organization Development* (Reading, Mass.: Addison-Wesley, 1973). Used by permission.

2. Conducting studies to ascertain optimal organization structure or management system design.
3. Develop and implement plans for initiating and maintaining organization or management system changes.
4. At management's direction, assess the effectiveness of designated corporate-wide or divisional programs with respect to their stated goals and objectives.
5. Identify and develop plans for increasing management effectiveness and improving work relationships.
6. Participate in the design or redesign of organizations or management systems.
7. Coordinate the implementation of newly established functions.

4. *Approach*

A. *To provide* an internal consulting resource to management.

1. To identify barriers to effective organization performance.
2. To analyze conditions which impact the organization and affect its performance.
3. To propose action plans which can resolve organization problems through effective problem-solving and decision-making.
4. To assist management in designing and implementing plans to resolve problems.

B. *To assist* client organizations in

1. Identifying and clarifying goals and objectives.
2. Identifying barriers to achieving goals and objectives.
3. Analyzing possible causes of continuing organizational problems.
4. Developing effective problem-solving mechanisms.
5. Designing and implementing plans to overcome problems identified.

5. *Typical Activities*

A. *Organization*

—analyzing functions (who does what)
—organization structuring
—identifying authorities and responsibilities
—job design and redesign

B. *Systems*
—mapping out the present
—identifying dysfunctions caused by duplication, omissions, inefficiencies
—planning for attaining system improvement

C. *Planning*
—identifying short-term and long-term goals and objectives
—anticipating problems
—developing plans to maximize organizational effectiveness
—improving communication, feedback
—enhancing problem-solving capabilities at lowest possible level

D. *Applied Research*
—analyzing policies, procedures, and practices of the client organization
—assessing organization effectiveness as it relates to its external environment, interfacing organizations, members' perceptions
—identifying or clarifying goals and objectives
—developing standards of performance
—examining management practices
-hiring
-promotion
-grievance handling
-etc.
—evaluate ongoing programs
-operating plans
-manpower plans
-succession planning
-minority programs
-high-potential programs
-professional development

6. *Procedures*

1. Ascertain the objectives of the project to be undertaken with the client.
2. Gather data that clarify the extent of the problems that relate to the project objectives.
3. Present preliminary findings to the client for further clarification and/or direction.

4. Propose a specific plan of action that will
   -clearly identify the problem
   -identify a feasible problem-solving model
   -implement proposed solutions
   -evaluate outcomes
5. Conclude the project when satisfactory results have been achieved.

7. *Specific Competencies*
   1. Problem identification
      -intrapersonal
      -interpersonal
      -interorganizational
   2. Data gathering
      -from surveys
      -from interviews
      -from existing historical data
      -etc.
   3. Data feedback
      -clarification of felt problems
      -climate analysis
      -management systems performance
   4. Design problem-solving models
      -appropriate to the situation
      -collaborative
      -participative (as appropriate)
   5. Develop action plans
      -specific to the task
      -supported by the client
      -within target dates
   6. Evaluate outcomes
      -consultant's actions
      -effectiveness of the project's design
      -establish criteria for evaluating effectiveness of action plans

In their book Margulies and Wallace cite several issues that internal consultants must face. They include:*

---

* Adapted from Margulies, N., and J. Wallace, *Organizational Change: Techniques and Applications* (Glenview, Ill.: Scott-Foresman, 1973).

1. *The general resistance to consulting help within an organization.* Generally there is resistance to such help based on the fact that the person who is in need of help does not recognize that he has a problem; therefore he resists any kind of approach from a consultant in an effort to help him.

2. *Differentiation and integration.* A consulting team working within an organization needs to keep in mind these two basic things. They serve as a switching center for information within the organization, transferring information from one place to another which can over a long period of time create difficulties within the organization. They, in other words, cannot always be the middleman to differentiate one part of the organization for the other. The second point is that they also serve an integrating function that is bringing people together or linking organizations which may not be working together effectively. Initially, an integrating function is extremely important; however, there is always a tendency when an outside group such as a consulting team comes in to help that the organization will become dependent and unable to work on its problems without the assistance of the consulting team.

3. *Relationships to external consultants.* Internal teams generally have problems working effectively without an outside consultant. It is almost essential in large OD projects to use outside help. The need for development of a meaningful relationship with the external consultants is essential if an OD team is established internally. This means that a contract needs to be developed which explains explicitly how the outside team is going to work with the inside team.

4. *Sustaining the change effort.* Very often the initial excitement, challenge and stimulation of trying to bring about effective change wears off and the OD efforts falter along the way. It is essential that an OD team working to bring about effective change recognize that it is a long-term effort and that they must constantly be guarding against the possibility of complacency and waning interest.

STEPS IN THE INSTALLATION OF AN OD EFFORT

As previously discussed, there are five basic steps in the OD process. Let us go over them again.

Step 1: *Recognition of the need for change.* This means looking for the manifest problems which point to the fact that a change should be made.

Step 2: *Development of an organizational strategy.* That is: Who is going to manage the process? Should we have an organizational development team? How is the team going to function? What steps are we going to take? With whom are we going to work? And within what kind of time frame are we working?

Step 3: *Diagnosis—data collection—interpretation.* In this step we are designing the ways in which we are going to collect information. These will tell us what is actually happening in the organization and how we will find out what the basic problems are.

Step 4: *Action planning.* In this case we take the information growing out of the diagnosis and interpretation of the information and design solutions to the problems.

Step 5: *Evaluation and monitoring of progress.* Although we have not spent a great deal of time talking about the evaluation and monitoring process, we believe that it is probably one of the most important parts of any OD intervention. The reason it tends to be neglected in our conversation, and probably is also neglected by others in the OD field, is because it is very difficult to do. Nonetheless, managers and OD practictioners attempting to carry out an OD intervention should establish evaluation and monitoring guidelines to be used to check the progress of the intervention.

CONDITIONS AFFECTING SUCCESS AND FAILURE OF OD PROJECTS

Richard Beckhard suggests several basic conditions which lead to failure in OD projects:*

1. A continued discrepancy between top management statements of values and styles and their actual managerial behavior.
2. The big program of activities without any solid base of change goals.

---

* Beckhard, R., *Organization Development: Strategies and Models* (Reading, Mass.: Addison-Wesley, 1969). Used by permission.

3. Confusion of the ends and the means. [That is, not always having ways of solving problems that are consistent with the end result desired.]
4. Short time framework. [Again, we would like to stress that OD is not a short-term project. It is long-term.]
5. No connection between behavioral-science-oriented change efforts and management-services/operations-research-oriented change efforts. [What Beckhard is suggesting here is that both the behavioral science or systems within the organization need to be integrated.]
6. Overdependence on outside help.
7. Overdependence on inside specialists.
8. A large gap between the change effort at the top of the organization and efforts in the middle of the organization.
9. Trying to fit a major organizational change into an old structure.
10. Confusing good relationships as an *end* with good relationships as a *condition.* [In other words, good relationships are an important condition in an effective organization, but they are not the end state.]
11. The search for "cookbook" solutions. [Trying to reach into the OD techniques barrel and pull out something that will work for you.]
12. Applying an intervention or strategy inappropriately. [Or using the wrong thing to solve the wrong problem.]

Beckhard goes on to point out that there are conditions which he believes are necessary for successful OD activities:*

1. There is pressure from the environment, internal or external, for change.
2. Some strategic person or people are "hurting."
3. Some strategic people are willing to do a real diagnosis of the problem.
4. There is leadership (consultant, key staff man, new line executive).

---

* Ibid.

5. There is collaborative problem identification between line and staff people.
6. There is some willingness to take risks in trying new forms or relationships.
7. There is a realistic, long-term time perspective.
8. There is willingness to face the data of the situation and to work with it on changing the situation.
9. The system rewards people for the effort of changing and improvement, in addition to rewarding them for short-term results.
10. There are tangible intermediate results.

OD PLANNING WORKSHEET

To conclude this book we have prepared a worksheet which you may wish to use as you consider the possibility of developing an OD project within your organization. This worksheet is designed to give you some ideas about the types of things you need to consider as you start your project. The topics listed in the worksheet have all been discussed in this manual. If you have questions, you are encouraged to go back to the sections of the book which apply to that particular topic.

OD planning worksheet

Dept./Unit/Organization ____________________

Time frame of intervention ____________________

1. Brief description of Dept./Unit/Organization involved.

____

____

____

____

____

2. Manifest signs of need for change (i.e., problems).

____

____

____

____

____

3. Available sources of data relative to the problem.

____

____

____

____

____

4. Data collection approaches (analysis of best approach to use).

	Approach	*Pro*	*Con*
a)			
b)			
c)			
d)			
e)			
f)			

Decision on approaches to use: ______________________________

____

____

5. Extent of commitment of organization to solve problem (including top personnel).

____

____

____

6. Need for outside consultation (consider complexity of problem, available inside competency, etc.)

7. How should you organize to conduct the OD project? (i.e., organize team, get total group involved, etc.)

8. How will you measure progress? How will you monitor progress?

9. What are the specific goals of the OD motivation? (What do you want to accomplish? What do you want to change?)

10. Other notations/consideration.

APPENDIX I

BIBLIOGRAPHY ON ORGANIZATION DEVELOPMENT

ARGYRIS, C., *Management and Organizational Development: The Path Xa to Yb* (New York: McGraw-Hill, 1971).

ADAMS, J. A., *Theory and Method in Organization Development: An Evolutionary Process,* Arlington, Va.: National Training Laboratories, Institute for Applied Behavioral Science, 1974).

BECK, A. C., and E. HILLMAR, *A Practical Approach to Organization Development Through MBO—Selected Readings* (Reading, Mass.: Addison-Wesley, 1972).

BECKHARD, R., "An Organization Improvement Program in a Decentralized Organization," *Journal of Applied Behavioral Science* **2,** 1 (1966), pp. 2–25.

———, "The Confrontation Meeting." *Harvard Business Review* **45** (1967), pp. 149–155.

———, *Organization Development: Strategies and Models* (Reading, Mass.: Addison-Wesley, 1969).

———, "Planned Change in Organizational Systems." Invited address presented at the meeting of the American Psychological Association, Miami Beach, Sept. 1970.

BEER, M., and E. F. HUSE, "A Systems Approach to Organizational Development," *Journal of Applied Behavioral Science* (1972), p. 8.

BEER, M., and S. KLEISATH, "The Effects of the Managerial Grid Lab on Organizational and Leadership Dimensions," in S. S. Zalkind (Chm), Research on the Impact of Using Different Laboratory Methods for Interpersonal and Organizational Change. Symposium presented at American Psychological Association, Washington, Sept. 1967.

BEER, M., G. F. PIETERS, S. H. MARCUS, and A. T. HUNDERT, "Improving Integration between Functional Groups." A Case in Organization Change and Implications for Theory and Practice. Symposium presented at American Psychological Association, Washington, Sept. 1971.

BENNIS, W. G., "Theory and Method in Applying Behavioral Science to Planned Organizational Change," *Journal of Applied Behavioral Science,* **1** (1965), pp. 337–360.

———, *Changing Organizations* (New York: McGraw-Hill, 1966).

———, *Organization Development: Its Nature, Origins and Prospects* (Reading, Mass.: Addison-Wesley, 1969).

BLAKE, R. R., and J. S. MOUTON, "Initiating Organization Development," *Training Directors Journal,* **19,** 10 (1965), pp. 25–41.

———, *Corporate Excellence through Grid Organization Development: A Systems Approach* (Houston: Gulf, 1968).

———, *Building a Dynamic Corporation through Grid Organization Development* (Reading, Mass.: Addison-Wesley, 1969).

———, L. B. BARNES, and L. E. GREINER, "Breakthrough in Organization Development," *Harvard Business Review* **42** (1964).

BLAKE, R. R., J. S. MOUTON, and R. L. SLOMA, "The Union Management Intergroup Laboratory: Strategy for Resolving Intergroup Conflict," *Journal of Applied Behavioral Science* **1** (1965), pp. 25–57.

BLAKE, R. R., H. A. SHEPARD, and J. S. MOUTON, *Managing Intergroup Conflict in Industry* (Houston: Gulf, 1964).

BUCHANAN, P. C., "The Concept of Organization Development, or Self-Renewal, as a Form of Planned Change," *Concepts For Social Change* (Washington: National Training Laboratories, 1967), pp. 1–9.

———, "Crucial Issues in Organizational Development," in G. WATSON (ed.) *Change in School Systems* (Washington: National Training Laboratories, 1968).

———, *Reflections on a Project in Self-renewal in Two School Systems* (Washington: National Training Laboratories, 1968).

———, "Laboratory Training and Organization Development," *Administrative Science Quarterly* **14** (1969), pp. 466–480.

BURKE, W. W., *Contemporary Organization Development: Conceptual Orientations and Interventions.* (Washington: National Training Laboratories, 1972).

CHASE, P., "A Survey Feedback Approach to Organization Development." In *Proceedings of the Executive Study Conference* (Princeton, N.J.: Educational Testing Service, Nov. 1968).

Cohen, A. M., and T. Petrella, "Power: What is the OD Consultant's Response to Separateness, Risk and Fight?" Paper presented at the Fall National OD Network Conference, New York, October 1971.

Davis, S. A., "An Organic Problem-Solving Method of Organizational Change," *Journal of Applied Behavioral Science* **3,** 1 (1967), pp. 3–21.

———, "Building More Effective Teams," *Innovation,* 1970, pp. 32–41.

Dayal, I., and J. M. Thomas, "Operation KPE: Developing a New Organization," *Journal of Applied Behavioral Science* **4** (1968), pp. 473–506.

Dunnette, M. D., and J. P. Campbell, "Laboratory Education: Impact on People and Organizations," *Industrial Relations* **8** (1968), pp. 1–45.

Dutton, J. M., review of R. R. Blake and J. S. Mouton, *Corporate Excellence through Grid Organization Development: A Systems Approach Administrative Science Quarterly* **14** (1961), pp. 608–610.

Dyer, W. G., R. F. Maddock, J. W. Moffitt, and W. J. Underwood, "A Laboratory-Consultation Model for Organization Change." *Journal of Applied Behavioral Science* **6** (1970), pp. 211–227.

Fordyce, J. K., "A Task-process Approach to Organization Development," in *Proceedings of the Executive Study Conference* (Princeton, N.J.: Educational Testing Service, Nov. 1968).

———, and R. Weil, *Managing with People: A Manager's Handbook of Organization Development Methods* (Reading, Mass.: Addison-Wesley, 1971).

French, W. L., and C. H. Bell, *Organization Development: Behavioral Science Interventions for Organization Improvement* (Englewood Cliffs, N.J.: Prentice-Hall, 1973).

Frohman, M. A., "An Empirical Study of a Model and Strategies for Planned Organizational Change," unpublished doctoral dissertation, University of Michigan, 1970.

———, and M. Shaskin, "The Proact of Organization Development: A Selective Review," unpublished manuscript, undated.

Golembiewski, R. T., *Renewing Organizations: The Laboratory Approach to Planned Change.* (Itasca, Ill.: F. E. Peacock, 1972).

———, and B. C. Stokes, "Planned Change in Organization Style Based on the Laboratory Approach." *Administrative Science Quarterly* **15** (1970), pp. 79–93.

———, "Planned Change Through Laboratory Methods," *Training and Development Journal* **27,** 3 (March 1973), pp. 8–28.

Goodacre, D. M., "Organization Development: The Name of The Game," *Training and Development Journal* **22,** 5 (May 1969), pp. 22–25.

HARRISON, R., "Training Designs for Intergroup Collaboration," *Human Relations Training News* **11,** 1 (1967), pp. 1–3.

HELLER, F. A., "Group Feedback Analysis: A Method of Field Research." *Psychological Bulletin* **72** (2), (1969), pp. 108–117.

HERMAN, S., and R. PHILLIPS, "Applications of Gestalt in OD." Workshop presented at Fall National E. D. Network Conference, New York, October 1971.

HORNSTEIN, H. A., and D. W. JOHNSON, "The Effects of Process Analysis and Ties to His Group Upon the Negotiator's Attitudes Toward the Outcomes of Negotiations," *Journal of Applied Behavioral Science Approach* (New York: The Free Press, 1971).

KURILOFF, A., *Organization Development for Survival* (New York: American Management Association, 1972).

LAWRENCE, P. R., and J. W. LORSCH, *Developing Organizations: Diagnosis and Action* (Reading, Mass.: Addison-Wesley, 1969).

LEAVITT, H. J., "Applied Organizational Change in Industry: Structural, Technological, and Humanistic Approaches," in J. G. MARCH (ed.) *Handbook of Organizations* (Chicago: Rand-McNally, 1965).

LIPPITT, G. L., "Emerging Criteria for Organization Development," *Personnel Administration* **29,** 3 (1966), pp. 6–11.

———, *Organizational Renewal* (New York: Appleton-Century-Crofts, 1969).

———, *Visualizing Change: Model Building and the Change Process* (Fairfax, Va.: Learning Resources Corporation, National Training Laboratories, 1973).

———, L. E. THIS, and R. G. BIDWELL, *Optimizing Human Resources* (Reading, Mass.: Addison-Wesley, 1971).

LORSCH, J. W., and P. R. LAWRENCE, *Managing Group and Intergroup Relations* (Homewood, Ill.: Richard D. Irwin, 1972).

MARGULIES, N., "Organizational Development and Changes in Organization Climate," *Public Personnel Management* **2** (March 1973), pp. 84–92.

———, "Implementing Organizational Change Through the Use of Internal Consulting Teams," *Training and Development Journal* **25,** July 1971.

———, and A. RAIA, "Action Research and the Consultative Process," *Business Perspectives* **5** (Fall 1968), pp. 26–30.

———, *Organizational Development: Values, Process, and Technology* (New York: McGraw-Hill, 1972).

MARGULIES, N., and J. WALLACE, *Organizational Change: Techniques and Applications,* Glenview, Ill.: Scott-Foresman, 1973.

MILES, M. B., H. A. HORNSTEIN, D. M. CALLAHAN, P. H. CALDER, and R. S. SCHIAVO, "The Consequence of Survey Feedback: Theory and Evaluation," in W. G. BENNIS, K. D. BENNE, and R. CHIN (eds.) *The Planning of Change,* 2nd. Ed. (New York: Holt, Rinehart & Winston, 1961).

———, "Data Feedback and Organization Change in a School System." Presented at the meeting of the American Sociological Association, August 1966.

MITCHELL, M. D., D. L. KOPPES, D. R. NEUKOM, and T. E. REAVIS, "Organization Development at Newark," unpublished report (Oakland, Cal.: Kaiser Aluminum & Chemical, 1971).

NEFF, F. W., "Survey Research: A Tool for Problem Diagnosis and Improvement in Organizations," in S. M. MILLER and A. W. GOULDNER (eds.) *Applied Sociology* (New York: Free Press, 1965).

PARTIN, J. J., "Organization Development: A Perspective," in *Current Perspectives in Organization Development,* J. J. PARTIN (ed.). (Reading, Mass.: Addison-Wesley, 1973).

SCHEIN, E. H., *Process Consultation: Its Role in Organization Development* (Reading, Mass.: Addison-Wesley, 1969).

———, and W. G. BENNIS, *Personal and Organizational Change Through Group Methods: The Laboratory Approach* (New York: John Wiley and Sons, 1965).

SCHMUCK, R. A., P. J. RUNKEL, S. SATUREN, R. MARTELL, and C. B. DERR, *Handbook of Organization Development in Schools* (Palo Alto, Cal.: National Press Books, 1972).

SHERIF, M., O. J. HARVEY, B. J. WHITE, W. R. HOOD, and C. W. SHERIF, *Intergroup Conflict and Cooperation: The Robbers' Cave Experiment* (Norman, Okla.: University of Oklahoma Book Exchange, 1961).

SHERWOOD, J. J., "Planned Renegotiation: A Norm-setting OD Intervention." Paper presented at New Technologies in Organization Development Conference, New York, October 1971.

TANGERMAN, E. J., "Every Man His Own Inspector, Every Foreman His Own Boss at Graflex," *American Machinist,* **7** (1953), p. 7.

TANNENBAUM, R., "Organizational Change Has to Come Through Individual Change," *Innovation* **23** (1971), pp. 36–43.

THOMAS, J. M., and W. G. BENNIS, *Management of Change and Conflict* (Baltimore, Md.: Penguin Books, 1972).

T.R.W. Systems Group, "Manager's Guideline—Organization Development," April 1969.

WAGNER, A. B., "The Use of Process Analysis in Business Decision Games." *Journal of Applied Behavioral Science* **1** (1965), pp. 387–408.

WALTON, R. E., *Interpersonal Peacemaking: Confrontations and Third-party Consultation* (Reading, Mass.: Addison-Wesley, 1969).

———, "Frontiers Beckoning the Organizational Psychologist." Invited address presented at the meeting of the American Psychological Association, Washington, September 1971.

———, and J. M. DUTTON, "The Management of Interdepartmental Conflict: A Model and Review." *Administrative Science Quarterly* **14** (1969), pp. 73–84.

———, and T. P. Cafferty, "Organizational Context and Interdepartmental Conflict," *Administrative Science Quarterly* **14** (1969), pp. 522–542.

WATERS, C. A., "Building Internal Resources for Organizational Development." In *Proceedings of the Executive Study Conference* (Princeton, N.J.: Educational Testing Service, November 1968).

WILSON, J. E., D. P. MULLEN, and R. B. MORTON, "Sensitivity Training for Individual Growth—Team Training for Organization Development," *Training and Development Journal* **22,** 1 (1968), pp. 47–53.

ZAND, D. E., "Collateral Organizations." Workshop presented at Fall National OD Network Conference, New York, Oct. 1971.

ZAND, D. E., F. I. STEELE, and S. S. SAKLIND, "The Impact of an Organizational Development Program on Perceptions of Interpersonal, Group and Organizational Functioning." In S. S. SALKIND (Chm.) Research on the Impact of Using Different Laboratory Methods for Interpersonal and Organizational Change. Symposium presented at the meeting of the American Psychological Association, Washington, September, 1967.

———, "Collateral Organization: A New Change Strategy," *Journal of Applied Behavioral Science* (Jan.–Feb. 1974).

APPENDIX II

OD TERMINOLOGY

Acceptance needs: A phrase applied to an individual, referring to his or her desire to be liked and accepted. It is usually prefaced by "high" or "strong," rarely by "low" or "weak," and is usually mildly derogatory of the person so described.

Achievement needs: A phrase applied to an individual, referring to his or her desire to perform work successfully. Sometimes implies that the person described as having "high" achievement needs cares more about getting work done and/or self-advancement than about the welfare of others. (See *Task-oriented.*)

Action research: A cyclical process of research-change-research-change, etc. The results of research produce ideas for changes; the changes are introduced into the same system and their effects noted through further research. The number of cycles may be infinite. Increasingly the phrase is used to describe what any action-taker in an organization does.

Adaptive: A term used to describe the behavior of many kinds of systems. Originally used mainly to describe individuals (e.g., "his adaptive behavior"), it is now also applied to groups and organizations vis-a-vis their environments. It is usually employed to summarize a number of specific actions or events (e.g., "Mrs. Y has a very adaptive style"), and hence its meaning is often vague.

Ambivalent: Literally, able to value something in two ways. It denotes an attitude or feeling that one holds or perceives another to hold. When it is a self-description, it may be a euphemism for, "I am confused," or "I disagree."

Authenticity: A technical term in existential psychology. Practically, it is synonymous with the colloquial phrase, "to be straight" with another person. It refers to one's openness and honesty and is sometimes used in a negative form ("He lacks authenticity") to describe another person's poor or tasteless behavior.

Back-home: The situation one has come from and will return to. It is used at *Off-site* conferences and retreats as a way of importing reality into the proceedings.

Behavioral science: The currently popular phrase for the various disciplines which study human behavior. As such, all of the traditional social sciences are included. Some argue that in the singular the phrase implies a spurious unity among these various disciplines. The phrase is also often capitalized; e.g., "The floor layout is consistent with findings from Behavioral Science." However, it is probably more appropriate to capitalize the phrase only where it is a proper name, as in, "The Behavioral Science Division of the Graduate School of Administration."

Body movement: The rapidly growing set of techniques aimed at making participants more aware of their own bodies and at connecting these new awarenesses to their present verbal interpretations of the reality around and within them. (See *Nonverbal, Self-awareness.*)

Boundary: A term used to describe processes in organizations which are conceived as *Systems* or as fields of interacting forces. Boundaries can be conceived in physical terms, as in a wall between two departments in an organization. More subtly, boundaries may be social processes, as in the boundaries between blacks and whites. Boundaries may be temporal: Things done at different times can be said to be bounded from each other. Any set of forces or factors which tend to differentiate parts of the system from each other can be said to have a boundary effect.

Bridging: Individual, group, or organization actions which aim to bring together elements in the system, or between the system and its environment, which are bounded from each other. An excellent example is the idea of an *Intergroup* and the actions which flow from it. Groups are bridged by considering them together as a larger entity.

Case method: A teaching technique which presents the learner with accounts of real events and challenges him or her to interpret them. It is popular in many business schools but less common among organization trainers because of the skills needed on the part of the instructor. It is one technique among many for increasing the involvement of the learners with the subject matter and with each other. (See *Experiential.*)

Catalyst: A term applied to a person, or to the role of a person, who is in the position of trying to make something happen without desiring and/or being able to command that it happen. This is typically a self-description, and it is often not clear what is being catalyzed.

Change agent: Individual (internal or external) engaged by the client organization to help the organization change.

Client system: The system (person, group, organization, etc.) which is the object of change efforts by some other agent. Often shortened to "the client." The client may be in the same organization as the consultant/ *Change agent,* as in the case of a line manager who is the client of a staff group, or the client and the consultant may be in different organizations entirely. One of the crucial ingredients of a change *Strategy* is asserted to be answering the question, "Who's the client?"

Clinic (to): Verb, meaning to focus on a specific problem or condition. A staff meeting may include clinicking as well as planning.

Clinical: A type of stance or orientation toward reality, usually including a desire to deal with wholes, not parts; concrete facts, not abstractions; and an intent to solve problems, not merely to analyze them.

Closed system (thinking, approach, etc.): The tendency to disregard relations between a system and its environment. This tendency often tends to be an unwitting simplification, and as such can lead to error. (See *Open system.*)

Closure (need for): A commonly felt need to see something finished, or brought to a logical endpoint. Sometimes it is used to describe a person who is uncomfortable with ambiguity and uncertainty.

Cognitive approach (style, level): Knowledge-oriented. It is a term applied to behavior which is comparatively intellectual and devoid of feeling. (See *Head level.*)

Communication (one-way, two-way): One-way communication describes an *Interaction* in which one or both parties are paying little attention to what the other is saying or doing. In two-way communication, presumably both parties are engaging and responding to each other. Technically there can be no such phenomenon as one-way communication.

Conflict management: a class of training techniques and concepts which purport to help trainees deal more effectively with *Interpersonal* conflict in organization situations. Particular stress is placed on *confronting* and *working through* conflict rather than avoiding it or trying to resolve it by fiat.

Conflicted (to be): To be in a state of conflict, especially to feel oneself to be in such a state.

Confront: A term referring to the process by which one person attempts to make another person aware of aspects of his behavior of which he seems unaware. It is used increasingly in the phrase, "a confronting style," to describe a person who habitually gives such *Feedback* to others.

Consortium: A group of consorts; an association of like-minded people. This is a somewhat precious term.

Consultant (internal, external): An internal consultant is a member of the organization he or she is attempting to influence, and may or may not have a job title which identifies him or her as an internal consultant. An external consultant is not a member of the system in any sense of employeeship. Much attention has been given lately to the problem of the distinctive opportunities and limitations of these two consulting roles. The consensus appears to be that, in the long run, effective *Organization Development* cannot be performed without *Inputs* from both positions.

Counterdependent: A technical term in personality theory, used informally to refer to one who consistently resists the authority, structure, and leadership of others.

Culture: A technical term with many and various definitions. It is used typically among practitioners, to refer to patterns of practices and attitudes which are—or seem to be—ingrained and difficult to change. Frequently employed in such phrases as: "the company culture" or "it is imbedded in the culture," etc.

Data-based intervention: Specific technique in Action Research. A data-based intervention follows some data collection phase and is an *Input* into the system using the data that have been collected. Alternatively, it can be the act of presenting the data to members of the system, thus initiating a process of system self-analysis.

Defensive: A technical term in personality theory, now widely used for any kind of resistant behavior.

Dependency: A technical term in personality theory, used informally to describe what seems to be an inordinate reliance on the ideas and strength of another. It is often used as "dependency needs." (See *Counterdependent.*)

Diagnosis: Among practitioners, a process of finding out what is going on in a *Social system* and interpreting the findings in light of the theories to which one subscribes. It is rarely used to refer to a formal process of research and analysis but rather to a more eclectic and impressionistic approach. (See *Sensing.*)

Dissonance: A term borrowed from the theory in psychology known as cognitive dissonance, which deals with the behavioral consequences of knowing two or more incompatible things at one time. Dissonance may be employed whenever the user senses incompatibility in people's points of view, as in: "I sense a lot of dissonance up and down the hierarchy." It may also be employed in self-description, as, "I have a lot of dissonance on this problem." (See *Conflicted.*)

Dyad: In psychology, two people and their dynamic interrelations; more informally, two people. Its usage has extended recently to "triad," or three people.

Dynamic(s): A term used very widely for any kind of process or set of forces. Its popularity is probably caused by the common desire not to appear to think in terms of static certainties. The thing or process described as dynamic is often left quite vague and ill-defined.

Dysfunctional: Those aspects of systems which work against the goals. This term refers to the "bad" parts of systems. (See *Functional.*)

Ecological: From ecology; the study of the relations between a system and its *Environment.* It is being used more and more loosely and hence is in danger of losing its meaning and becoming a camouflage for vagueness.

Empathic: From "empathy"; to be able to project oneself into another and hence understand him or her. It is used relatively interchangeably with "sensitive" and "understanding." It sometimes appears as the variant term, "empathetic."

Encounter: A term that has become generic for the entire collection of techniques which aim to bring people into closer and more intimate relations. For example, *Encounter group.*

Encounter group: A small group of persons meeting with the intention of (1) seeking deeper and more personal relations among members and (2) learning more about themselves and others from the attempt to develop these relations. (See *Sensitivity training; T-group.*)

Entry process: Jargon phrase for the highly complex set of enabling conditions by which a *Consultant* begins to exert influence. It is regarded as a highly important set of actions separate from the main work the consultant intends, although they are naturally closely related.

Environment: Used to refer to the physical and social context within which any target system is functioning, be it a person, group or organization. (See *Ecological.*)

Existential: From the philosophy of existentialism. It is used informally to refer to facts or processes which seem inevitable or virtually unchangeable. It is sometimes redundant, as in "the existential fact."

Experiential: A term for a kind of learning process in which the content of what is to be learned is experienced as directly as possible, in contrast to being read about in a book or talked about in lecture and discussion. The term applies to a wide variety of training techniques. It is often used in the phrase, "experiential level," in contrast to *Cognitive level.*

Expert power: A technical term from leadership literature, referring to the influence a person has in a situation by virtue of his or her technical or professional expertise.

Facilitate: A verb referring to a process by which events are "helped to happen." "Facilitating" is a kind of influence role which is neither authoritarian on the one hand nor abdicative on the other. In self-description, the term can sometimes be a euphemism for an intent to be more directive.

Family group: A type of training group in which participants have a familial relationship and in which the focus of the group's work is this relationship. It may be an actual family, or it may be a work group in an organization.

Feedback: Technical term from systems theory, used primarily to describe one person's report to another of the effect of his or her behavior on the reporter. "Negative Feedback" is a disapproving report. "Positive Feedback" is the opposite. The term is also used for larger-scale systems; e.g., feedback from the market to an organization.

Field: A technical term in perceptual psychology: the totality of persons, things, and events in awareness at a given time. It is used loosely to refer to what the speaker reports being aware of, such as, "My field is very much focused on profits right now."

Fishbowl: An *Experiential* training technique in which some members of a group sit in a small inner circle and *Work-the-issue,* while other members sit in an outer circle and observe. It is useful as an intergroup training technique. Sometimes each member of the outer group is instructed to observe a particular member of the inner group.

Follow-on experience: A phrase referring to a carefully planned activity that follows and reinforces training.

Formal (leader, organization, system): A term introduced originally in the Hawthorne studies to designate the set of organizational relationships that were explicitly established in policy and procedure (i.e., the "formal organization"). Now the term "formal" has been prefixed onto many types of organizational phenomena, but the reference to what is established in policy and procedure remains. "Formal leader," the designated leader of a group, whether he or she has the most influence in it or not, is one of the most common phrases which derive from this term. (See *Informal.*)

Freeing-up: Jargon, referring to the process by which an individual is able to become less *Defensive,* more open, more free. It is related to Kurt Lewin's use of the term "unfreezing" to describe the first step in any change process.

Functional: Describes those parts of a system that promote the attainment of its goals. The term derives from a mode of analysis in psychology and sociology (which took the approach from the biological sciences) that seeks to understand systems by understanding the effects that parts of the system have on each other and the mutual effects between the system and its environment. These effects are regarded as functions and dysfunctions. More informally, the two terms are used in place of "good" or "bad."

Games: (1) Games may refer to patterns of *Interpersonal* behavior that are highly stable and recurrent. (The implication is that patterns so labeled are somehow pathological.) (2) Kinds of *Experiential* techniques for making various phenomena more real and immediate. Games have been employed, for instance, in *Simulation* of conflict and bargaining, leadership struggles, group norms, etc.

Gatekeeping: A term from group dynamics that describes a person in a group who regulates *Interaction* patterns by asking people for their ideas, suggesting to others that they talk less, etc.

Gestalt: A school of thought in pyschology. Phenomena are studied and interpreted as patterned wholes rather than as aggregates of parts. It has had major effects on contemporary personality theory. It is now used as a shorthand way of referring to an overall view of anything: a "big picture" approach; e.g., "My gestalt on the issue is . . ." It is also used increasingly to refer to a collection of techniques which are purported to help people to identify and then reorganize their own gestalt of reality.

Goal-setting: Beyond its literal meaning, this phrase frequently denotes a process which occurs at someone's suggestion early in the life of a group. Hence it is a kind of agenda item.

Grid: Shorthand for "Managerial Grid," a popular *Organization Development* program originated by Blake and Mouton. The basic diagnostic step of the program is to locate each participant on a 9 × 9 grid, the axes of which are "concern for people" and "concern for production." Other common phrases are "grid work," "grid lab," "grid OD."

Group maintenance: Those behaviors exhibited by members of a group which are *Functional* for holding the group together, increasing members' liking for each other, and differentiating the group from its environment. When one member is very prominent in this process, he or she is said to be playing a group-maintenance role.

Growth: A widely used term, reflecting the concern of theorists and practitioners for improvement in personal, group, and organizational behavior. Constantly in danger of becoming an ideological cliche. Identification of growth stages, rates, and directions is a major focus of contemporary theory and research.

Gut level: Jargon for statements that describe feelings or emotions, in contrast to *Head level.*

Head level: Jargon for statements and behavior which have no apparent feeling content, in contrast to *Gut level.*

Helping relationship: Deriving from the "client-centered" therapies introduced by Carl Rogers and others. It is usually employed to describe a relation one intends to establish in order to assist another to increase his or her ability to cope. It is distinguished from other possible relationships which one could establish with another person; e.g., a *Power-based* relationship, a casual friendship, etc.

Here-and-now: A phrase describing the temporal focus of attention. It is typically employed to forestall a reworking of past events or an over-planned concern for the future. Shorthand reference to the complex of perceptions presently existing among a set of people.

Homeostasis: A biological term for the tendency of living systems to regulate and balance themselves. It is employed widely as a quasi-description of social phenomena. It is increasingly used as a term of disapproval as concerns for growth and change become dominant.

Influence: The effects people have on each other, intended and unintended. The term has debatable meaning, however, since personal values intrude. Influence is often seen to be at odds with a *Helping relationship,* somehow not *Facilitative,* perhaps somewhat Machiavellian. Others argue that "influence" is a useful generic concept and as such does not deny the possibility or value of help and benevolence.

Informal (leader, organization, system): A term introduced in the Hawthorne studies to designate the set of organizational relationships which emerge over time from the day-to-day experiences people have with each other. Informal relationships are expressive of the needs that people actually feel in situations, in contrast to the needs their leaders think they should feel.

Input: A term from system theory used to describe people's contributions to a system, particularly their contributions of ideas.

Interaction: Virtually any behavior resulting from interpersonal relationships. In human relations it includes all forms of communication, verbal and nonverbal, conscious and unconscious. Interactions speak louder than words.

Interface: Jargon from the aerospace industry and systems engineering, used both as a noun and a verb to describe one or more *Interactions.* It is commonly used in describing work-related interactions among groups.

Intergroup: An important class of intra-organization relationships, such as between departments. It is used primarily as an adjective, although some are trying to establish "intergroup" as a noun.

Intern experience: An opportunity to work in a learner's role while yet engaged with real organizational problems under conditions of personal responsibility. It is recognized as an important step in the training of *Change agents.* More and more organizations are creating such roles for their employees and for students from universities.

Interpersonal: The generic term for relations between persons, usually two. It is a prefix for many phrases, such as "interpersonal relations," "interpersonal aspects," "interpersonal conflict," etc.

Intervention: A somewhat precious term for any action on the part of a *Change agent,* popular among some theorists of the organization change process. Intervention carries the implication that the action is planned and deliberate, and that presumably it is *Functional.*

Intrapsychic: Phenomena which occur within the person, particularly feelings. It is usually not employed in reference to thoughts, ideas, or beliefs. The term is often used when the intent is to stress the invisibility and inaccessibility of events within the person.

JABS: *The Journal of Applied Behavioral Science,* published quarterly by the NTL Institute for Applied Behavioral Science.

Job enlargement: A phrase invented by Charles Walker of Yale University to describe the process by which jobs are redesigned to make them more complex and, presumably, more interesting. The aim is to make the task more of a "natural whole" to the man performing it. Job enlargement has been applied most commonly to so-called blue collar jobs.

Job enrichment: A phrase invented by Herzberg to describe the process by which more factors which have a truly motivating effect are built into a job. Herzberg's theory of "motivating" factors and "hygiene" factors is the basis for the technique.

Judgmental: Jargon for the process of making evaluations of a person or event. It is typically used in a faintly derogatory sense, as in: "He should have just listened, but instead he became pretty judgmental."

Lab: A shorthand term for any of a wide variety of programs which derive from the so-called "laboratory method of training," an approach that is primarily *Experiential.* The term "lab" has become a suffix for many specific types of training designs; e.g., "conflict lab," "personal growth lab," etc.

Learning community: A popular phrase for all types of assemblages in which the main objective is learning. The phrase implies, additionally, that the teachers or trainers are learners themselves. The ingredients of a learning community are not spelled out anywhere but are instead a set of ideas and practices from diverse sources. Lacking such a specification of its nature, it is likely that the phrase will be overused and will eventually become an euphemism for classroom.

Linking pin: A term for a role described by Likert. The key function of the person in this role is to maintain lines of communication between parts of the organization. A linking pin may operate up and down a hierarchy or across hierarchies. The role may be provided for in the *Formal* organization, but more commonly it is *Informal.*

Management by objectives: A management strategy developed by Odiorne which makes the establishment and communication of organization objectives the central function of a manager. It is based on the assumption that supervision and leadership will work best under conditions in which both superiors and subordinates have prior "contracts" (i.e., agreements about directions, priorities, and objectives.

Matrix: A bivariate cross-classification system, such as a two-dimensional grid. Beyond the technical meaning of this term in mathematics and its derivations in the engineering sciences, it is being used increasingly whenever two variables and their interactions are described. The recent rash of two-dimensional theories (e.g., Blake, Herzberg, McGregor) and the temptation to express these theories in a pseudoscientific two-coordinate geometry probably has led to this usage of the term.

Mechanistic: Having a machine-like quality—predictable, artificial, contrived. It is applied to a wide range of phenomena, from a single person's style to the policies of an organization; it is virtually always denigrating.

Microlab: A simulation of *Sensitivity training* in which the pace of events is speeded up by putting the group under intense time pressure. It is a technique widely employed as an *Experiential* introduction to various group methods.

Model: A simplification of some phenomenon for purposes of study and understanding. The concrete embodiment of a theory. Behaving in an idealized way so that others might learn or change their behavior through identifying with and adopting those behaviors displayed.

Mutual influence: The condition in which all parties to an action have some control over its conduct and outcome. It is considered by many to be always preferable to unilateral influence, although research does not bear this out. (See *Communication; Ownership.*)

Needs: A central concept in psychology referring to all of the biological and psychological requirements for the maintenance and growth of the human animal. It is employed among practitioners chiefly to refer to those psychological needs which are and are not met in organizational life, with the emphasis on the search for ways that more needs can be met.

Need hierarchy: A particular theory about the operation of needs in the organism, introduced by Abraham Maslow. The major assertion is that classes of needs are arranged in a hierarchy, with the most basic biological needs at the bottom and the more variable psychological needs near the top. The theory says that "higher" needs cannot be activated until "lower" needs are relatively satisfied. The theory has led to a variety of shorthand phrases for describing "where a person is" in the need hierarchy at a given time; e.g., "esteem level," "social level," "security level," etc. This particular theory also was the basis for McGregor's *Theory X—Theory Y* formulation.

Network: An increasingly common term for talking about a large set of individuals who are in regular touch by virtue of some common set of interests. They need not belong to the same organization. To say that a person is "in the network" is to say not only that he or she is in communication, but also that his or her values and behavior are somehow *Organic* in relation to the others. It is a modern variant of the older phrases, to be a "member of the club" or to be "one of the boys (girls)."

Nondirective: The name for a method of interviewing first introduced by Carl Rogers. The patient in therapy is in charge of the pace, content, and direction of the interchange. The term is now used to refer to any similar approach used by any power figure; e.g., a teacher or a consultant.

Nonverbal: In addition to its literal meaning, the term has become a label for the growing number of training techniques which do not use language. (See *Body movement, Experiential.*)

Norms: Rules regulating behavior in any *Social system*. They are usually unwritten and are more specific and pointed than "values," in that deviations from norms are followed by such punishments as kidding, the silent treatment, or, in the extreme, banishment.

NTL: National Training Laboratories, now renamed the NTL/Institute for Applied Behavioral Science. It is a prominent training and consulting organization known for its use of group methods.

OD specialist: A nascent, somewhat precious term for one who consciously practices various OD approaches and techniques. Many OD specialists actively avoid getting tagged with this title.

Off-site: Away from the regular place of work, as an off-site *Lab.* (See *Back home.*)

Openness: Accepting the communications and *Confrontations* of others and expressing oneself honestly, with *Authenticity*.

Open system: The tendency to take into account relations between a system and its environment. This concept in systems theory is borrowed from the biological sciences. It refers to the nature and functions of transactions that take place between a system and its environment. (See *Closed system.*)

Organic: Having a natural and real aspect—uncontrived. It is the opposite quality of *Mechanistic*. It is also used in speaking of particularly close and interdependent relations between people. "Organic" is widely employed as a desirable quality of human relationships, especially in organizations.

Organization Development (OD): An evolving collection of philosophies, concepts, and techniques which aim at the improvement of organization performance by intervening in *Social systems*. Attempted changes may be directed at individuals, *Dyads*, groups, *Intergroups*, *Formal* structures, or *Cultures*. OD is not yet a coherent applied science. It derives more from the social than the biological or physical sciences.

Ownership: Jargon for the quality of being personally committed and hence presumably entitled to influence in a situation, as in: "I feel some ownership in this program."

Participant-observer: A type of role wherein the person is involved in a *Social system* as a member but is also studying and evaluating it by another set of criteria as an observer. This dual role may or may not be known to other members of the system. The role of participant-observer is widely identified as desirable and strategic, but it has been performed successfully by comparatively few people.

Participative: A term used to describe those techniques employed by a power figure which aim to involve subordinate, lower-power persons in the decision-making process of an organization. For example, "participative management." The aim is to increase the sense of *Ownership* at lower levels.

Planned change: The generic phrase for all systematic efforts to improve the functioning of some human system. It is defined by Bennis to be a change process in which power is roughly equal between changer and changee and in which goals are mutually and deliberately set.

Policy science: A phrase for those social sciences whose theories and research findings have implications for developing policy guidelines for the management of human systems.

Post-industrial society: A phrase applied to Europe and the U.S. in the last third of the Twentieth Century, in which the problems of production have been solved. By implication, it is a society now confronted with questions of priority, ecological balance and justice.

Power-based: Reliance on force or its residues, status and position. It is a disapproving phrase, as in: "power-based solution," or "power-based approach."

Proactive: Initiating, starting. This adjective is frequently used in tandem with its opposite, "reactive."

Problem-solve: A verb used to describe a process of resolving everyday issues between people in work situations. It implies focusing on the concrete and the relevant. This is an important element in *Organization Development* work reflecting the idea that if an *OD specialist* can't help people in *Working through* their real operating problems, his or her reason for existing in this role is questionable.

Process: A generic term for the way any system is going about doing whatever it is doing. "Social process" is the way persons relate to one another as they perform some activity. Most training techniques aim, in one way or another, to make people more sensitive to "social process." The phrase, "process level" refers to the events occurring within the social process.

Reentry: Jargon for the process of moving back into one's work situation from a temporary training setting, which may or may not have involved a "trip to the moon." The term refers to an increasingly urgent issue as training environments diverge more and more from work environments. (See *Back home*: Off-site.)

Resistance to change: Virtually a cliché for what people supposedly do when someone attempts to change their behavior. Although considerable research has been done on the causes and conditions of resistance to change, comparatively few of these nuances have found their way into practice.

Rogerian: Pertaining to the ideas of the psychotherapist, encounter group facilitator, and theorist, Carl Rogers. (See *Helping relationship, Nondirective.*)

Role: A position in a *Social system* with certain responsibilities and functions. A role may be established in the *Formal* system, or it may have emerged from operations and be *Informal.* It is used in a huge variety of phrases, such as: "helper role," "dependent role," "role conflict," "role ambiguity."

Self-actualization: A phrase quite widely used to refer to the process by which an individual reaches the highest level of functioning of which he or she is capable. More concrete definitions are difficult in that, theoretically, self-actualization is different for every person. Self-actualization is the top level in Maslow's *Need hierarchy.*

Self-awareness: A positive goal of most training techniques which aim at behavior change. Self-awareness means becoming aware of one's existing patterns of behavior in a way that permits a relatively nondefensive comparison of these with potential new patterns.

Self-concept: A major theoretical notion in many personality theories. It refers to the picture one holds of oneself—who I am—often a hardly articulate collection of feelings, hopes, and beliefs. A major object of *Self-awareness* is to identify one's self-concept more accurately and completely.

Self-organizing system: A technical term in biology, now used more loosely to refer to any system which maintains a continuous balance of internal forces and continuous balance with its environment without major changes in its energy sources. Also, it is a system which achieves this condition by itself without assistance from forces in its environment.

Sensing: Jargon to describe a *Diagnosis* process under conditions in which the needed information, such as attitudes, is intangible and elusive.

Sensitivity training: The collection of methods for improving the individual's sensitivity to him- or herself and others. Although a large number of variations exist, the common ingredients seem to be: (1) the guidance of a trained person or persons; (2) intense *Interpersonal* experience by the trainee; (3) a relatively protected environment, free from ordinary pressures and distractions. The *T-group* is the classical, but not the only, means of achieving these three conditions.

Simulation: The creation of "working model" of some system, so that the key elements and their *Interactions* are highlighted. It refers to an important class of training techniques in which trainees are able to experience various dimensions of organizational behavior in a *Lab* context.

Skill training: Training that is concerned more with improving effectiveness than learning concepts. It is often used in a mildly negative way to explain that some particular type of training program is "not merely" skill training.

Social leader: The person who performs the *Role* of leading a group in nonwork activities. (See *Group maintenance.*)

Social system: Any set of persons and their relationships. More narrowly, it refers to the pattern of social relations existing within a *Formal* organization. The phrases "social organization" and "social grouping" are sometimes used to refer to smaller-scale social systems.

Socio-technical system: This concept refers to the same concrete phenomena as *Social system* but by the inclusion of the term "technical" emphasizes the physical realities of the system and the *Technologies* it employs to do work.

Stranger lab: A type of *Sensitivity training* experience in which the members are not acquainted with each other at the outset.

Strategy: A term employed to discuss the larger-scale plans a *Change agent* may have for changing a system, a planned sequence of *Interventions*. It is also used when explaining the choice of one approach or technique over another.

Structural (focus, approach, emphasis): Jargon for a change *Strategy* that focuses on the *Formal* organization. A structural approach may concern itself with organization charts, job descriptions, and assigning authority to roles. It assumes that behavior change will follow. This is a particularly important class of *Interventions* when the target for change is an entire organization.

Survey-feedback: A type of *Data-based intervention* which flows from surveys of the members of a system on some subject and reports the results to the group. It is a useful *Intervention* when problems are widely shared but when each person feels rather alone.

Synergy: Originally a term for the combined and cooperative operations of the bodily organs. Now it is a jargon for any process in which more is accomplished by cooperation than could be done by separate efforts.

Systemic: A jargon term meaning "in the system" or "of the system." It is often redundant, as in "systemic interrelationships," "systemic interactions," etc.

T-group: Training group, a type of group which is not structured at the outset by any person or agency but which rather evolves its own structure. The task is for members to learn about themselves in a social context. The evolving structure is continuously examined by looking at the social *Process* of the group. The T-group is helped in this by a *Trainer*. Usually a series of meetings is held. The goal of such groups is behavior change on the members' parts. Evidence is presently mixed about the type and degree of changes which tend to occur. (See *Encounter group, Family group, Lab, Microlab, Sensitivity training, Team* building.)

Task group: A group of people who work together.

Task leader: A role which commonly emerges in any group. The task leader is the person who exercises the most influence on the way the group attempts to accomplish its main task.

Task-oriented: A person who is strongly interested in accomplishing the tasks of his or her *Social system*. When applied to a person, the phrase may be mildly critical. (See also *Achievement needs.*)

Team (building, development): The process by which work relations are improved among members of some *Task group* in an organization. Various techniques from *Sensitivity training* may be used. It is a major overall *Strategy* in *Organization Development.*

Technology: A standardized, communicable process for doing work. It is identified with machinery in many instances, yet it is broader than this. It is used increasingly in *Organization Development* to refer to ways of making *Interventions,* as in "*Team* building technology."

Temporary system: A relatively new phrase which refers to *ad hoc* task forces of various sorts which are formed around specific problems in or across organizations. Members of a temporary system are often relative strangers.

Theory X—Theory Y: Two practical theories of human motivation in organizations, developed by McGregor. Theory X is essentially a set of negative and diminishing assumptions about man; Theory Y is a set of positive and enhancing assumptions. Very different managerial behaviors are presumed to follow from the two sets of starting assumptions. McGregor and many subsequent theorists have strongly advocated Theory Y. The two approaches, per se, are now somewhat in eclipse as the degrees of oversimplification they contain become clearer. Yet the spirit that runs through Theory Y is still strongly present in *Organization Development.*

Therapy: A technical term for the professionally directed improvement of the physical and mental functioning of a person. It is now often used much more loosely to describe any event which, somehow, makes things better for a person or for a group.

Trainer: Besides its generic sense of "one who trains," it refers to one who conducts *T-groups* and other kinds of *Labs.*

Trust level: A phrase for the degree of mutual trust among a set of persons. Raising the trust level is usually a major goal of *Team* building.

Work-the (-problem, -issue, -relationship, etc.): Jargon for the process of engaging an issue and trying to resolve it, as opposed to talking around it without ever surfacing the real concerns.

Working-through: A phrase for the process by which *Interpersonal* relationships are diagnosed and then improved. A great deal of working-through takes place, for instance, in *Team* building.

APPENDIX III

RESOURCE MATERIAL FOR OD INTERVENTIONS

1. *A Handbook of Structural Experience for Human Relations Training*
   Pfeiffer and Jones

Vol. I	1969	Vol. IV	1973
Vol. II	1970	Vol. V	1976
Vol. III	1971		

   University Associates
   P. O. Box 80637
   San Diego, Calif. 92138

2. *Organization Psychology—An Experiential Approach*
   Kolb, Rubin, McIntyre, 1971
   Prentice-Hall, Inc.
   Englewood Cliffs, N.J.

3. *Management—An Experiential Approach*
   Knudson, Woodworth, Bell, 1973
   McGraw-Hill, Inc.
   1221 Avenue of the Americas
   New York, N.Y. 10020

4. *NTL, Trainer Exercises*
   NTL Institute for an Applied Behavioral Science
   1201 16th Street, N.W.
   Washington, D.C. 20096

5. *1972, 73, 74, 75, 76, 77 Annual Handbook for Group Facilitators*
   Pfeiffer and Jones
   University Associates
   P. O. Box 80637
   San Diego, Calif. 92138

6. *An Experiential Approach to Organizational Development*
   Harvey and Brown, 1976
   Prentice-Hall, Inc.
   Englewood Cliffs, N.J.

7. *Organization Behavior in Action—Skill Building Experiences*
   Morris and Sashkin, 1976
   West Publishing Co.
   50 Kellogg Bldg.
   St. Paul, Minn. 55102

APPENDIX IV

CHANGING LIFE STYLES

The term "life style" refers to individuals in terms of their actions and thoughts which are partly unique to them and partly shared with others. Life style is a product of one's own culture and one's own deliberate choices, and is often studied by looking at a number of different value/behavior dimensions. These dimensions represent various aspects of life which are likely to be dealt with in varying ways, depending on the particular society or organization involved. One dimension, for example, would be the nature of the relationship between father and son; another would be the meaning and significance of work, and so on.

Life style can be classified into three basic groups. The earliest of these Life styles, referred to as *Formalistic,* was prevalent around the turn of the century. This life style, which still prevails today, emphasized rationality, control, and order in one's life. It developed along with, and was fostered by, the traditional, bureaucratic model of organization.

Generally, as technological changes became more rapid, and organizations became more complex, a second life style began to emerge. Shortly after World War II, people began to recognize the social nature of man. Within the behavioral sciences an entirely new field emerged, called Group Dynamics. Out of this social, interpersonal group context, industrial humanism—or "human relations," as we know it today—developed. This new model of organization stressed personal growth, human dignity, work satisfaction, and democratic processes through various collaborative, interpersonal and group relationships. It also fostered the *Sociocentric* life style.

After World War II, advances and technology for the production of goods and the communication of information led to a society which became much more prosperous, as we all know, and a much better informal society than ever known in the history of the world. This increase in wealth and information led to the emergence of a still different life style, referred to as the *Personalistic* life style. This particular life style, accepted by many of our younger people today, is often idealistic and emphasizes personal choice and responsibility along with an integration of all aspects of one's life.

The accompanying table outlines how different life styles react and feel about various dimensions or aspects of life.

The Values and Resulting Behavior of Three Life Style Classifications

Values/Behavior	Formalistic	Sociocentric	Personalistic
Antecedent of Action	Direction from authorities	Discussion, agreement with others	Direction from within
Form of Control	Rules, laws, rewards, punishments	Interpersonal commitments	Action congruent with sense of self
Information for Control	Rules, laws, authorities' wants	What "We" think and feel	What "I" think and feel
Object of Responsibility	Superordinate powers	Peers, colleagues, self	Self
Desired End	Compliance	Consensus, agreement	Actualization of individual
To be Avoided	Deviation for authoritative direction	Failure to reach agreement	Not being one's self
Material Goods	Compete for means of control	Collaborate for means of control	Take for granted
Use of Experience	Validate external order	Share for agreement and growth	Define self
Basis for Growth	Following the established order	Interaction	Acting on awareness of self
Position Relative to Others	Member of hierarchy	Peer group member	Separate individual
Interpersonal	Structure oriented	Group oriented	Individual oriented
Time Perspective	Future	Near future	Present

INDEX